Talking Walls
The Stories Continue

Teacher's Guide

Margy Burns Knight
Thomas V. Chan

with details from the original *Talking Walls: The Stories Continue* illustrations
by Anne Sibley O'Brien

Tilbury House, Publishers
Gardiner, Maine

Tilbury House, Publishers
2 Mechanic Street
Gardiner, ME 04345
800–582–1899 • www.tilburyhouse.com

First Edition 1996

10 9 8 7 6 5 4 3

Design: Edith Allard, Crummett Mountain, Somerville, Maine
Layout: Nina Medina, Basil Hill Graphics, Somerville, Maine
Editors: Jennifer Elliott and Mark Melnicove
Publisher: Jennifer Elliott
Marketing and Publicity: Michelle Gifford
Office Manager: Jolene Collins
Warehouse: William Hoch
Printing and Binding: Bookcrafters, Fredericksburg, Virginia

Cover illustration by Anne Sibley O'Brien. Students in Kent Clady's sixth grade class at the John Marshall Middle School in Indianapolis, Indiana, studied walls in a social studies unit, with the book *Talking Walls* as their focal point. As a community service project, they offered to repair the entrance wall at a nearby apartment complex. The six graders worked hard, scraping and painting the wall. The residents of the apartment complex were so pleased with the students' work that they contacted local T.V. stations and even invited the six graders to use their pool at the end of the school year for a cookout.

Contents

Introduction

"When you change the telling of the past,
You actually change the present."
— David Muro

Welcome to *Talking Walls: The Stories Continue Teacher's Guide*. Once again, Tom Chan and I offer you an extensive menu of activities for students in grades three and up as they explore the walls in my new book, *Talking Walls: The Stories Continue*. If you choose to use the book for younger students, I suggest that you use it as a picture book by telling students some of the stories and encouraging them to retell them in their own words.

Talking Walls: The Stories Continue can be used by you and your students as a storybook, a picture book, or a history book. Most of the activities can be used across several grade levels. This guide focuses on developing listening, thinking, communication, and writing skills. Many of the activities in Part I are adapted from the ideas of teachers who have used my first book, *Talking Walls*, in their classrooms.

We hope you and your students enjoy exploring and learning about the walls in the book, and that the following activities launch endless discussions and projects.

—Margy Burns Knight

Acknowledgements

Special thanks to the following readers: Mara Burns, Farida Alam-Huda, Susan Neyer, Anne Stauffer, and Kent Clady. Many thanks to Peggy Fucillo for helping with the bibliography.
—Margy Burns Knight

I would like to thank Debbie, my wife, for her encouragement and tireless effort in spending endless hours assisting me with research throughout this project and revising the manuscript to its polished and user-friendly conclusion.

Talking Walls: The Stories Continue gave me an opportunity to gain an empathic insight into the plights and injustices suffered by people all over the world, particularly the children of the world.

To the loving memories of the young children who were murdered in Dunblane, Scotland on 13 February 1996; to those who became innocent victims in the senseless conflicts in the former Yugoslavia and the former Soviet Union; to the rising hope for the children of Tibet, Northern Ireland, and Mexico; and to our own in North America, I affectionately dedicate my work.
—Thomas V. Chan

Talking Walls

The Stories Continue

Teacher's Guide

Part 1 Over the Walls

Part I introduces themes that connect many of the seventeen walls in *Talking Walls: The Stories Continue*. These are activities that encourage students to ask more questions, do their own research, and create projects that can take them beyond the text and pictures in the book.

Many of these activities can also be used with the fourteen walls featured in my first book, *Talking Walls*: The Great Wall of China, Aborigine wall art, the Lascaux Cave paintings, the Western Wall in Jerusalem, Mahabalipuram's Animal Walls in India, Muslim walls, the mysterious granite walls of Great Zimbabwe, the walls at Cuzco, Peru, the Taos Pueblo in New Mexico, the murals of Diego Rivera in Mexico, the design of the Canadian Museum of Civilization, the Vietnam Veterans Memorial, Nelson Mandela's prison walls, and the Berlin Wall.

—Margy Burns Knight
Winthrop, Maine
August, 1996

1. Questions

While I was researching and writing the book, I spent several days in classrooms listening to questions. I showed students a picture of a wall I was researching and told them a brief story based on what I knew about it so far. Then I asked them to ask me questions about each wall. I encouraged them to go beyond who-what-where questions. One way you can do this is by introducing Bloom's Taxonomy. As you introduce each wall, a list of questions could be posted as they are asked in the classroom, introducing and/or reviewing the six levels of questioning:

Knowledge: What? Where? Why? And when did...? Can you recall...? Can you list...?

Comprehension: How would you compare? How would you rephrase the meaning? What is the main idea? What can you say? How would you summarize?

Application: How would you show your understanding of...? How would you use...? What facts would you select to show? What examples can you find to...?

Analysis: Why do you think...? How would you categorize...? What conclusions can you draw? What is the theme?

Synthesis: What would happen if...? Suppose you could...? What facts can you compile? How can you improve...?

Evaluation: What is you opinion of...? What would you select? How would you compare the ideas, people...? Would it be better if...?

I haven't listed all the questions or key words used to elicit questions. A great guide is the *Quick Flip Questions for Critical Thinking* by Linda G. Barton, published by EduPress.

2. What Is a Wall?

Put this question in a visible spot and ask students to respond to it. You may want each student to write a response before you discuss it, or you could wait until after the discussion. Some students may want to change their responses after the discussion or when they have finished reading the book.

3. Illustrations

Encourage your students to spend time looking at the illustrations before they read the text. Ask them who and what they see, and what is happening in the picture. Where is the wall and what story is being told? Have your students write several questions about a favorite illustration. Students could pair up and ask each other questions. As a group, questions about each illustration could be asked and answered. Students could write a story about an illustration. They could also create dialogue for people in the illustrations.

4. Geography

Before the text is read, hold up each illustration and ask the students to guess where it is. (You can give clues.)

Make a list of all the countries represented in the book.

Put up a World Map in your classroom, and then ask students to look for articles about the countries they have listed. Post the articles near the map and have students give news briefings. Invite people from your community to your classroom who have traveled to or are from these countries.

Ask students what they know about each country and keep the responses visible around the classroom. Ask them what they would like to know about these places and how they think they could find the information. Books for each country could be collected and displayed near the map. You'll find many possibilities in the catalogs of Lerner Publications or Steck-Vaughn/Raintree.

References:

Grammar, Red. *Teaching Peace*, Smilin' Atcha Music, Red Note Records, 5049 Orange Port Road, Brewerton, NY 13028. "Places In The World" is on this cassette, and it is a great song for learning geography.
Chapin, Tom. *Mother Earth*, Sundance Music, Inc. "The Picnic of the World" is a song on this cassette that is also wonderful for teaching geography.

5. Tourist Brochures

Have students choose a wall that they would like to travel to sometime in their lives. It would add excitement if choices could be top secret as students produce brochures or posters or bumper stickers to show off their walls. When all students have finished, they could present their work to the class and see who else hopes to travel to the same place.

6. Travel Agent

Students become travel agents for one wall area. Other students call them and ask questions about a trip to that area. The travel agent would need to be well versed not only in the wall, but costs, distance, food, language, etc. You could have students build a travel agency out of refrigerator boxes, so turns could be taken as travelers and agents. Invite a travel agent into your class so students can ask questions. Involve parents and community members who come to visit the travel agency.

7. Passports

Invite people in from the community to show and share their passports. Are U.S. passports like all other passports? Why are they different colors or shapes? Do they all have similar information?

Have students make their own passports; as they travel to the countries in the book, they can have them stamped.

8. Newspaper

Have students write, design, and illustrate a newspaper about walls around the world.

9. Dress Up, Skits, Plays

Children in England dress up once a year as Hadrian's soldiers. Could your students reenact Hadrian's time? Could they write a play and build the wall? What other walls in the book could be reenacted in a play?

10. Animals

How many times are animals mentioned in the text? What animals live near each wall and why? How are the animals in Moscow the same or different than animals on Angel Island near San Fransico? Projects could be created about the habitats of the areas surrounding each wall.

References:

Brenner, Barbara. *Chibi: A True Story from Japan*, Clarion (New York), 1996. The true story of a duck named Chibi who lives in Tokyo. Chibi is the *Make Way for Ducklings* of Japan.
Brown, Ruth, *Ghost of Grey Friars Bobby*, Dutton (New York), 1996.
Wardweller, Frances. *Riptide*, Philomel, 1990. The story of a dog who saved a swimmer and became a "lifeguard."

11. Weather Report

USA Today has a great weather page. Using this and other sources, have students give weather reports for each wall area. Use graphs and charts to compare temperatures and climates. Have students pick their favorite climates and make posters announcing them.

12. Papier-Mâché

Students may want to re-create some of the walls in the book or create their own out of papier-mâché. The following recipe is easy for students to use:

Ingredients and Materials

1/2 cup of flour	shallow bowl, spoon, and measuring cup
3/4 cup of water	newspaper cut into one-inch strips

1. Put flour in bowl, add just 1/2 cup of water, and stir. (Keep the leftover water in case the paste gets too thick.) The paste should have the consistency of heavy cream.
2. Lay one strip of newspaper at a time into the paste mixture. Then hold it up with one hand and squeeze the excess paste out with the other hand.
3. Place the strips over a form, one at a time. The form can be made out of cardboard, crumpled newspapers, or anything else that approximates the basic shape you want. Keep adding strips, building and molding layers to achieve the final shape you want.
4. Let the papier mâché dry at least overnight. Don't paint it until it's completely dry.

13. Other Materials

Have students design walls using different kinds of materials. Cloth, paper, and yarn are some suggestions. They may also want to experiment with natural colorings and dyes such as tea and beet juice.

14. Rice Flour Wall Paintings

Using rice flour, water, and an array of brushes and sponges, students can create beautiful art on the exterior cement walls of their school. I did this with my children's classes. The younger class decided they wanted to do animals, so they did sketches of the animals before they made the paint. The older students decided not to have a theme, but made several sketches of ideas. Some students used brushes and other used their hands as they painted with rice flour paint. (Experiment with the amount of water to get the right consistency, and stir frequently.) The white paint showed up quite well and stayed until it faded with the rain and wind.

15. Refrigerator Boxes

Many students have used refrigerator boxes to build walls. Students could pick a wall and working in a group, re-create it with a refrigerator box. In one school I visited, all the walls were displayed in the gym when they were completed.

16. A Kindness Wall

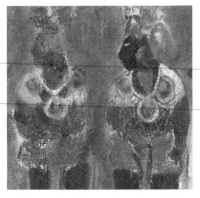

Kindergarten and second grade children in Haverford, Pennsylvania, built a Kindness Wall. Once a week, a second grade buddy writes a note to his or her kindergarten buddy and leaves it in one of the personalized envelopes that are part of the wall with students' names on them. The kindergarten buddy leaves a note or picture for his friend, too.

17. Walls in the Community

Brainstorm with your students about walls in your community. Where are they and what stories do they tell?

You can start the discussion with some of the questions on the endpapers. With the assistance of parents and community members, photos could be taken and displayed as a photo-essays

18. Religions

What religions are discussed in the text? How are they the same and different? What does religion have to do with the walls in the text? Without religion would there be the Peace Lines or painted walls at Divali? Invite to the classroom people from the community who have been to these walls or who practice one of the religions mentioned.

References:

Jacobs, William Jay, *Great Lives: World Religions*, Atheneum Books for Young Readers, 1996. This is a useful book aimed at intermediate students.
My Friends' Beliefs, Religions of the World Series, Silver Burdett, Morristown, New Jersey.
Pandell, Karen, *Learnings from the Dalai Lama*. Dutton Children's Books (New York), 1995.

19. What Will Happen?

What will happen in Northern Ireland? Students may want to organize a debate or a series of discussions on the issues in Northern Ireland. Invite people into your class who can tell both sides of the story. Similar projects could be done with other walls. Have the students look through the book and write other "What if?" questions.

20. Other Walls That Divide

Have students identify other walls that separate people. What do these walls look like? Why and when were they put up? Will they come down? Are there invisible walls that separate people?

References:

Fenner, Carol, *Randall's Wall*. Bantam Skylark (New York), 1992. Randall, a fifth grader, has built an invisible wall around himself, and his classmate Jean tries to break through it. A great read-aloud book.

21. Favorite Wall

I am often asked by students and teachers if I have a favorite wall. I tell them that the Vietnam Veterans Memorial Wall in Washington is my favorite because it inspired me to write my first book, *Talking Walls*. You could ask students to write one sentence about their favorite walls without using the words "favorite," "because," and "like." Encourage them not to tell anyone which walls they've picked. Then ask some or all students to share their wall stories. At the end, tally up the responses.

22. What If?

What if Hadrian's wall was never built or the Maya had never painted their murals? Have students write What if? questions for the walls and try to answer them.

23. Math

Have students go through the book and write down all the numbers. This could be done as a class, in small groups, or as a homework assignment. Put the numbers up in a visible place in the classroom so you can discuss them. What stories do the numbers tell? Ask students to graph or chart them into categories such as dates, distance, age, length.

In *Talking Walls* I wrote that the Vietnam Veterans Memorial wall is 185 giant steps long. If a giant step is three feet long, how long are the walls in the book? A poster or bulletin board could be created by students showing the relative size of the walls, using drawing to scale (e.g. 1 inch=10 feet).

24. Matrix

Students could choose a number of walls in the book and do a matrix project. They could include: materials, size, length, age, country, reasons for building, climate, current use, etc.

25. Going Into the Community

The cover of the book shows a group of sixth graders repairing a wall in their neighborhood in Indianapolis. Are there walls near your school that need repair or could use a mural?

26. Water

How often is water mentioned in the text and compendium? How is water said in different languages? Where is the fresh water of the world? What are the stories about? Was water used to build any of the walls? Are there lakes, rivers, or oceans near any of the walls? What role do these bodies of water play in the area? These questions could be used to launch discussions. Students could pair up and make posters or prepare reports. Someone may want to research local water issues and share them with the class.

27. Flooding

Ask some of these questions: Are there other countries or communities that are threatened by or victims of flooding?

Bangladesh has suffered greatly from flooding. Will dikes be built there?
Venice, Italy, has a unique system of canals. Why?
Are there positive aspects of flooding?
Are there negative aspects of building levees and dikes?

References:

Everett Fisher, Leonard. *Kinderdike*, Macmillan, New York, 1994. Based on a legend about a town in the Netherlands that was rebuilt after a terrible flood. This is a great read-aloud for younger children.

28. People

Who are the people mentioned in the text and compendium? List the names on the board before the text is read.

Ask students what they know about Neruda, the Dalai Lama, etc. Ask students what they would like to know about these people and how they would like to share their information. Some students may want to design a poster, and others may wish to do oral reports or research papers.

29. Shoeboxes and Milk Cartons

Have students collect milk cartons and shoeboxes and build the wall of their choice using them. Students could work alone or in groups. Each wall could be displayed. I have seen wishing walls, walls of dreams, walls of wisdom, and walls of peace made from milk cartons and shoeboxes. The writing could include information that was found in the text and new information about the wall that was found from another source.

30. Languages

How many languages are mentioned or written in the text?

What languages are spoken at the walls and by the people who live in each country?

A language wall could be built in your classroom starting with the languages spoken in your classroom and school. People from your community could be invited to share languages and add to the language wall.

31. Journals

Ask students to keep personal journals of the walls they "discover" during the year. A classroom journal of all the walls the students "collected" during the year could also be created.

32. Murals

Have students design murals of each wall in the book. These could be displayed together on a wall in the school.

33. Rewrite

A third grade class greeted me with a wall of their own words when I arrived in their classroom. They had each picked a wall in *Talking Walls* and rewrote the text in just three sentences. They told me that it wasn't easy taking all my information and trying to write it more concisely. They were pleased to hear that I do the same thing, many times, as I write my books.

34. Monuments

What is a monument? Are any of the walls monuments? Why do people build monuments? Are there monuments in your community? Does your community need a monument?

As you and your students discuss these walls, you could read *The Monument* by Gary Paulsen to them. It is the story of a town that needed a monument. The main character is a twelve-year-old girl. Students who are interested in monuments could research and report on monuments in your community.

References:

Paulsen, Gary, *The Monument*. Bantam Doubleday Dell (New York), 1991. "A powerful, affecting story with its comments on art and homage." *School Library Journal*.

35. Preservation

What does preserve mean? Are the walls in the books preserving anything? Why or why not?

These questions could begin many discussions. Start with your own community. Are there any places or things that have been preserved? What and why? You could ask a local historian to visit your classroom.

36. Festival of Lights

Divali is celebrated in the U.S. by many Hindu Indian Americans. Invite an Indian American into your class to tell about this colorful celebration. Are there other festivals, holidays, or celebrations in which lights have a special significance? Where and why?

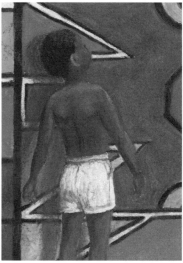

References:

Deshpande, Chris. *Diwali*. A and C Black (London), 1994. Shows children preparing for and celebrating Diwali (Divali) at school and at home.
Gilmore, Rachna. *Lights for Gita*. Tilbury House, Publishers (Gardiner, Maine), 1994. Gita celebrates Divali in her new home in North America.

37. Ndebele Classroom Wall

Decorate a classroom or hallway wall, Ndeble style. Students could work in groups to divide patterns and shapes. They could also make some of the paint from natural dyes.

References:

Angelou, Maya. *My Painted House, My Friendly Chicken, and Me*. Clarkson Potter (New York), 1994. Thandi, a Ndebele girl, tells about her life.
Courtney-Clarke, Margaret. *Ndebele*. Rizzoli (New York) 1986. A photo-essay book about the Ndebele people. Many stunning photographs of wall designs.

38. Storytelling Area

With the help of parents or volunteers, create a storytelling area in your classroom. A partition or wall could be built around the area. Students could gather to talk about the importance of storytelling and tell stories. Why has storytelling been such a popular way to pass down history? Has it only been done in Morocco?

Invite parents and employees from the area to come in and tell a favorite story.

39. Poetry

Doug Rawlings, whose poem inspired me to write *Talking Walls*, is a co-founder of Veterans For Peace. This group, which started in Maine, has chapters throughout the U.S. and in England, Canada, and Israel. Their Maine address is: Box 4313, Portland, ME 04112. Below is Doug's poem:

> The Wall
> (to Jerry Genesio)
> Descending into this declivity
> dug into our nation's capital by
> cloven hoof of yet another one
> of our country's tropical wars
> slipping past the names of those

whose wounds refuse to heal
past the panel where my name
would have been
could have been
perhaps should have been
down to the Wall's greatest
depth where the begiining
meets the end
I kneel
Staring into the wall
through my own reflection
beyond the names of those who
died so young
And now that wall has finally found me
Fifty eight thousand
thousand yard stares
have fixed on me
As if I were their polar star
as if I could guide their mute testimony
back into the world
as if I could connect
all those dots
in the night sky
as if I could tell them the reason why.

What is this poem about? What stories does it tell? Is there other poetry in the book? What did Pablo Neruda write about in his poems? What did the immigrants on Angel Island write in their poems? Poems about the poems in the book or poems about walls could be written by students and displayed. Invite a poet into your class to read his or her poetry and talk about poetry.

40. Haiku

Haiku poetry is three lines. The first line has five syllables, the second has seven syllables, and the third line has another five syllables.

Students could write Haikus before and after they read the text.

41. Cinquain

There are several ways to write cinquains. This version has four lines. The first line contains one word, a noun. The second has two adjectives describing the noun. The third line has three "-ing" words describing the actions of the noun. The fourth is a synonym for the initial noun.

Cinquains could be written after your students define a wall, but before they look at the text. Another one could be written about a specific wall in the book.

42. Odes

Pablo Neruda wrote hundreds of odes. An ode is a poem that usually expresses praise. William Wordsworth, Percy Bysshe Shelley, John Keats, and Alfred Lord Tennyson were other writers who published odes. Have your students read a few of Neruda's odes and then write their own. Ask them to write odes about each wall.

References:

Neruda, Pablo. *Odes to Opposites*. Little Brown (Boston), 1995.

Neruda, Pablo. *Odes to Common Things*. Harcourt, New York, 1992. These odes are about everyday events in children's lives.

Roman, Joseph. *Pablo Neruda*, Chelsea House (New York), 1992. This is a biography of Neruda for older students.

43. Acrostic Poems

Write poems vertically. Each line begins with a different letter and forms a word or phrase. You could write acrostic poems for each wall or country in the book.

44. Hunting for Poems

With the help of parents or the school librarian, set up a display of poetry books. Then have students "hunt for poems." Each student could look for a favorite poem to bring to class and write on a "wall-fence" that symbolizes the one around Neruda's home. After they write the poem, they could continue by writing a message to the poet whose work they chose, or to another poet. Students could continue to hunt for poems and keep a personal anthology.

45. Materials

There are seventeen walls discussed in the book. What materials were used to build them or used to tell their story? How much of this information is in the text? With your students, list the information available in the text. When the list is complete, ask students what is missing and how could they fill in the blanks. Also, what else could they learn?

Have students look at the list of materials that has been posted in the classroom. Ask them if any materials on the lists are used to build local walls. Some students may want to find out how many different materials are used to build walls in your community. You could invite a builder or contractor or mason into your class.

46. Governments

The king of Thailand had the learning walls built at Wat Po, Neruda spoke out against the government of Chile, Emperor Hadrian had a wall built in England, and the British army built the Peace Lines in Belfast, Northern Ireland.

Ask your students what they know about the present governments of the countries in the text. Keep this list up in the classroom.

Ask them to write questions about what else they may want to know about these governments. How are these political systems similar and different?

Have any of these governments changed since the wall was built? If so, how?

Students could role-play different systems of government. Invite people in from the community who have lived in countries whose governments are not like the U.S.

47. Political Leaders

What leaders are mentioned in the book? What roles did/do they play?

Students could write news releases about each leader and zap them through some kind of space machine to introduce them to the class. They may want to begin: "As a child...."

Would the political views of these leaders be accepted today?

Who are the present political leaders of the countries mentioned in the text? What roles do they play? Have students find pictures of these leaders and keep them posted in the classroom. Ask students to keep their eyes open for articles about these leaders. Post any article next to the picture.

A news hour could be written and produced to introduce these leaders to the class.

When your students are familar with these leaders, they could be asked to support or criticize their policies.

Further Teaching Resources

The Spirit That Moves Us: A Literature-Based Resource Guide: Teaching about Diversity, Prejudice, Human Rights and the Holocaust. For grades K-4: Maine Holocaust Human Rights Center, Box 825, Palermo, Maine, 04354; 207-993-2620. Also available from Tilbury House, Publishers. A similar resource guide for grades 5–8 will be available from Tilbury House in May 1997.

Teaching Tolerance is published by Southern Poverty Law Center, 400 Washington Avenue, Montgomery, AL 36104. It's a great resource for teachers and parents.

Rethinking Schools, 1001 E. Keefe Avenue, Milwaukee, Wi. (414-964-9646) This educational journal is packed with new ideas, book reviews, and references.

Insight Guides, Houghton Mifflin, Boston. These up-to-date travel guides are like mini history books. A librarian at Harvard told me about them.

The Institute For Peace and Justice, 4144 Lindell Blvd., St Louis, MO 63108. Publishes a newletter and curriculum guides.

Asian American Studies Curriculum Resource Guide. Massachusetts Asian American Educators Association, Cambridge, 1995. To order the guide, contact: Dr. Peter Kiang, U. Mass. Boston, 100 Morrissey Blvd., Boston, MA 02125; 617-287-7614.

Parry, Caroline. *Let's Celebrate, Canada's Special Days*, Kids Can Press, Toronto, 1987.

Stoodt, Barbara D., Linda B. Amspaugh, and Jane Hunt, *Children's Literature: Discovery for a Lifetime*, Gorsuch, Scarisbrick Publishers (Scottsdale, Arizona) 1996. A rich resource for teachers and librarians.

Part 2 Within the Walls

Talking Walls: The Stories Continue is a treasury of fine lessons on multiculturalism, world issues, and history. It is also a jubilant celebration of diversity in today's world culture, imparting optimism in the human journey. This part of the *Teacher's Guide* provides practical teaching ideas, hands-on learning experiences, resource references, explanatory notes, background information, and Internet links on the subjects being explored.

In scope and sequence, the activities are designed to be incremental in levels of learning, within each subject heading, progressing from simple to complex, concrete to abstract, and comprehensive to evaluative.

As far as possible, the activities provide students with an opportunity to extend their learning beyond the text in an active, multi-sensory, and interdisciplinary manner. They integrate subject areas in a multicultural context, such as language arts, science, social studies, mathematics, food experience, arts and crafts, and computer technology, just to name a few. Many of the activities are designed for students to construct meaning for themselves as they are guided to explore the subject matter. I trust that the activities suggested in this part of the *Teacher's Guide* will be a valuable and enjoyable companion to *Talking Walls: The Stories Continue* for you and your students.

—Thomas V. Chan
Winnipeg, Manitoba, Canada
August, 1996

About the Internet Resources

It is important to note that the Internet is fluid, constantly changing and growing. For this reason, it is possible that a URL (address for a particular site and abbreviation for Uniform Resource Locator) may change. If this occurs, use the key words of the title or name in a search engine (Lycos, Web Crawler, etc.) to relocate the site. Take, for example, the Internet resources for Morocco. For Activity #13, type "One and Only Morocco" (quotation marks included, which indicates that you are looking for this exact phrase) in the space marked "Search For." The search engine will hunt for this phrase and provide a list of all documents that include it. Activity #15 in this section has no title, so to search for this, type "King Hassan II" to probably find more than the site listed in this guide—but if this one still exists, it should be there. You could define your search more specifically by typing :Morocco + "King Hassan II" (the plus sign indicates that you are looking for a document that includes both the word "Morocco" and the phrase "King Hassan II"). Additionally, since more and more sites are being added every day, there is a very good possibility that, by using a search engine, you may find other excellent information on Morocco, or any other subject of this guide, on the Internet.

A word of warning: The Internet can quickly lead children to inappropriate material, and its use should always be carefully monitored. If you always make using the Internet an interactive process between yourself and your students, you will be able to supervise this resource appropriately.

The Internet is an exciting and extremely useful tool for research in the classroom. I hope that if you have never tried this medium before, you will "bite the bullet" and do so now. Your students, and you, will find a whole new world opened before them.

Wall 1 Morocco: A Crossroads of Many Cultures

Pre-Reading Warm-Up

1. The Camel: The Ship of the Desert:

"Walls that are as high as three camels surround Fez, a city in Morocco." An average camel stands 7 feet (2 meters) tall, taller than the average North American person. The wall that surrounds the old city of Fez is approximately 21 feet (6 meters) in height.

   Some of your students may not be familiar with the camel. A few may not know what the animal looks like. Using information from the "Teacher Notes" or from an encyclopedia, plus pictures you may glean elsewhere, share your knowledge about the camel so they can better appreciate the size of the walls of Fez (see also the Science activity on camels later in this chapter).

Language Arts

2. Folk Literature: Fairy Tales, Legends, and Folk Songs

"In the shadows of the ancient walls, the very young and the very old never grow tired of listening to the legends and folktales of the land they love."

   Folk literature is an entire canon of facts, thoughts, and emotions expressed in both the oral and written traditions by the people who love their land. Every country has its folk literature in all forms: music, songs, poetry, prose, drama, tales, fables, and legends, just to name a few.

   Explore with your class the folk tales, legends, fairy tales, folk music, and songs of the North American culture. Identify, list, and read or play to the class the poems, plays, tales, and songs that are used to express our heritage and culture. Below are some examples.

Folk Songs:
"This Land is Our Land" by Pete Seeger
"Green Leaves of Summer" by The Brothers Four
"Red River Valley"
"Tom Dooley" by The Kingston Trio
"Battle Hymn of the Republic"
"Ghost Riders in the Sky"
"Battle of New Orleans"
"Four Strong Winds" by Ian and Sylvia
"Cruel War"
"If I Had a Hammer"
"Canadian Railroad Trilogy" by Gordon Lightfoot

Poems:
"Casey at the Bat" by Earnest L. Thayer
"The Road Not Taken" by Robert Frost
"In Flanders Fields" by John McCrae
"The Shooting of Dan McGrew " by Robert W. Service
"Richard Corey" by Edwin A. Robinson
"Little Boxes" by Malvina Reynolds
"Happiness" by Carl Sandburg

"Cremation of Sam McGee" by Robert W. Service
"Superman" by John Updike
"Hollow Man" by T. S. Elliot
Fairy Tales, Folk Tales, and Legends:
Legend of the Sleepy Hollow
Paul Bunyan
Johnny Appleseed
Pinocchio
Bigfoot
Thumbelina
Peter Pan
The Ground Hog and His Shadow

3. Comparing Folktales

Read to your class two western and two North African (or Arabic) folk/fairy tales. Discuss how these tales are different from and similar to each other.

4. Creative Writing

Ask each student to create a fairy tale, either from scratch or to change a traditional fairy tale by telling it from a different point of view. For example, tell the Cinderella story from the point of view of the stepmother, recount the events in Jack and the Beanstalk by the giant, or rewrite the story of Red Riding Hood from the wolf's perspective. This could also be done as a group activity.

Social Studies

5. Moroccan Fest

Organize a "Moroccan Fest." If Moroccans live in your area, invite them to participate, otherwise make this part of a research project. Present the sights and sounds of Morocco through pictures, slides shows, videos, movies, and recorded music. Samples of Moroccan foods may be prepared either with prior arrangements with your guest speakers, or by your students with the help of their parents. (One recipe is provided later in this chapter.) For more Moroccan recipes, go to this Internet site:
URL: *http://maghreb.net/morocco/cuisine/*

6. Compare and Contrast Markets

"Not far from these noisy markets where everyone seems to be making, selling, or buying something, storytellers recite their tales."

Marketplaces in the Old World are more than a place for buying and selling. They also serve, in most cases, as places of social interactions and cultural displays. In Morocco, a rural market is called a soulk, and it is a characteristic feature of Moroccan life.

On chart paper, draw two columns with the heading of "Moroccan Market" on one and "Our Market" on the other. Help your students to compare and contrast a Moroccan market with our typical urban marketplace called a mall. Discuss the merits and disadvantages of each kind of market.

When this exercise is complete, direct your students' attention to the markets within the Milecastles dotted along Hadrian's Wall in Northern England. Help them to visualize what kind of activities might have taken place 2,000 years ago in Roman Britain. Encourage students to use library reference books for this exercise.

7. Geography

Morocco is a country of diversity: ocean, mountains, desert, and farmland. First inhabited by Berbers, the Phoenicians, Carthaginians, and Romans all had some influence in Morocco, but it wasn't until the Arabs spread across North Africa in an attempt to convert the world to Islam that real changes became permanent. At the turn of the century, Europeans took hold, with France being the dominant power until independence in 1955.

Morocco must import food and fuel because it cannot produce enough for itself. Much of the farming is done by hand still; fishing is important and the waters teem with fish. Tanneries in Fez, leather, clothing, and textiles are all important industries. The marketplaces or soulks are the center of village life. The predominant religion is Islam, and the country has a vital heritage of art with the mosques beautifully decorated and jewelry and even carpets all works of art.

Ask your students to locate Morocco in the atlas (or on a wall map). Explore with them the history of the country, the way of life in Morocco, Moroccan cultures, languages, and religions.

To provide ownership for and excitement in their learning, instruct students to call up or write to local travel agencies, Moroccan consulates, and business representatives, either locally or overseas, for tourist information on visiting Morocco. The following addresses may be useful for this project. (See, also, the bibliography at the end of this chapter.)

In the USA

Embassy of the Kingdom of Morocco
1601 21st Street NW
Washington, DC 20009
USA
Ph. (202) 462-7979; Fax (202) 265-0161

Morocco National Tourist Office
421 N. Rodeo Drive
Beverly Hills, CA 90210
USA
Ph. (310) 271-8939; Fax (310) 271-4817

Moroccan Tourist Office
20 East 46th Street
New York, N.Y. 10017
USA
Ph. (212) 557-2520

In Canada

Embassy of the Kingdom of Morocco
38 Range Road,
Ottawa, Ontario
Canada
K1N 8J4
Ph. (613) 236-6164; Fax (613) 236-7391

In Morocco

Office National Marocain du Tourisme
31 Angle Avenue al-Abtal and rue Oved Fas,
Agdal, Rabat
Morocco
Ph. (7) 775-171; Fax (7) 777-437

See also the sites listed under "Internet Resources."

Science

8. The Camel

Ask your students what they know about camels and list their information on the chalkboard. What else would they like to know about camels? Ask them how they'll find the answers to their questions, and list this information, too. After they've had a chance to do their research, ask them to share their information with pictures, reports, or role-playing.

Mathematics

9. Measuring and Estimating:

Form groups of three with your class. Ask students to measure a classroom wall with a yardstick or meter stick. Use a piece of colored chalk to mark off units of a foot or a meter. Because a student is not tall enough to measure the wall all the way to the ceiling, ask him/her to make the best estimation for the remaining upper part of the wall.

On the chalkboard, write down the findings of the groups, so that a comparison may be made. Ask the students to present the group findings in a graphic format, such as a bar graph. With the use of a measuring tape, take the measurement of the classroom wall (the regular modern-day classroom is about 12 feet or 4 meters tall), and place your finding on the chalkboard. Reinforcing the students' knowledge and skills in measurement and estimation, ask those groups whose estimations are far off to measure and estimate again. This second opportunity will help them to practice their skills in forming visual concepts.

Arts and Crafts

10. Create a Travel Wall Mural

Provide your class with a long sheet (approximately 9 feet or 3 meters, or longer) of white art project paper (it comes in a roll) and ask the students to create a Wall Mural of Travels.

The mural will be a collage of drawings, paintings, travel photographs, pictures from travel brochures, and magazine cut-outs that represent each student's (and your own) travels. Display the mural in the hallway adjacent to your classroom.

Explore with your class what they would need to do to be prepared for a visit to Morocco.

11. Sculpting

As an art project, ask students to make models of camels using either papier maché (see Activity #12 in Part I) or sawdust-flour dough (recipe in the "Teacher's Notes" in the chapter on the Dog Wall).

Food Experience

12. Recipe:

Dining in Morocco is an elaborate affair full of beauty and ritual. If you are a guest in a Moroccan home, you will be seated on a large, low couch and given cushions to place behind you and under one elbow to ensure your comfort. Servants, or a younger family member, will bring in special basins over which you may wash your hands. The basins are often works of art with the center raised to hold a cake of soap. Water is poured over your hands, and towels are supplied for drying. The master of the house begins the meal with the phrase, "Praise be to God," and then the meal begins, the order of dishes never changing. First comes a pastry which combines savory meat with sweet ingredients. Next, roast lamb followed by stews of various meats and/or vegetables (or fruit). Couscous is a traditional grain dish which often contains meat, vegetables, and/or a spicy sauce. It is expected that you eat some of everything offered; utensils are not used for eating at all except occasionally for couscous, which can be messy. At the end of the meal the water kettle, basin, soap, and towel are brought in again. Then begins the mint tea ritual. This tea, the national beverage, is always served after meals. If you ask for seconds your host will be flattered.

Moroccan Tea

To serve this in true style, the Moroccan host uses one tray (usually brass) to hold the teapot and small squat glasses, and a second, smaller tray on which sits three boxes containing the tea, sugar, and mint. A brass samovar, beautifully designed, is used for boiling the water.

Ingredients:

4 tsp. green tea (decaf)

1/2 cup sugar

1-1/4 cup firmly packed fresh
  spearmint leaves (other kinds
  of mint may be substituted)

Method:

1. Rinse a 4-cup teapot with boiling water.
2. Place tea, sugar, and mint into the empty teapot.
3. Cover with 4 cups boiling water.
4. Allow tea to steep at least 3 minutes.
5. Stir slightly and correct for sweetness.
6. Serve hot in glasses.

Note: For variation, add fresh orange blossoms to the pot before pouring in the boiling water.

Internet Resources

13. The One and Only Morocco

URL: *http://maghreb.net/morocco/*

This excellent site provides the following:

Historical Events

- The Green March (the peaceful retaking of Spanish Sahara);
- In the Middle of the Roman Empire: Volubilis;
- History of the Flag of Morocco;
- Historic Monuments; and
- Others.

Moroccan Cities (including Fez, and photos thereof);

Culture and Leisure

- Traditional Moroccan Craftworks (photos and explanations);
- Moroccan Cuisine (includes recipes);
- Picture Gallery (9 rooms of 16 photos each);
- Soulks (descriptions);
- Audio Clips of Moroccan Music (see "Moroccan Auditorium");
- and Sporting Activities.

Practical Information

- City Maps (including Fez);
- Moroccan Dictionary (short):
- Tourist Information; and
- Weather (general information plus link to Intellicast forecast for Casa Blanca).

14. *http://www.ic.gov/94fact/country/165.html*

This site contains facts about Morocco and includes a map.

15. *http://www.pitt.edu/~figtree/morocl.html*

Here you can find a photo of King Hassan II.

Teacher's Notes

Facts about Morocco

- *Official Name:* The Kingdom of Morocco (al-Mamlakah al-Maghribiyah)
- *Joined* the League of Arab States in 1958
- *Gained independence* from France on March 2, 1956
- *Political Capital:* Rabat
- *Commercial and Industrial Center:* Casablanca
- *Summer Capital:* Tangier
- *Traditional Capitals:* Marrakech, Fez (Fes), and Meknes
- *Government:* Constitutional Monarchy
- *Administrative Regions:* 37 provinces and 5 municipalities
- *National Day:* March 3, commemorating the anniversary of King Hassan II's accession to the throne
- *Legal System:* an eclectic system based on Islamic law and the French and Spanish civil codes
- *Official Language:* Arabic; French and Spanish are widely spoken as well
- *Official Religion:* Islam
- *Geography:* situated at the northwestern tip of Africa, where it faces northward across the Strait of Gibraltar to the continent of Europe, westward to the Atlantic Ocean, and northeastward to the Mediterranean Sea. Two mountain chains run through Morocco: er-Rif rises along the northern coast, and the Atlas divides the country topographically.
- *Berber:* They are the original inhabitants of Maghreb. During the time of the Roman colonization, Berber people were never quite conquered by the Roman invaders. Neither were they subjugated by Arabs and Islam. Most Moroccans are Berber by birth. The ethnic difference between the Arabs and Berber today is more linguistic than racial. The Berber language, although greatly influenced by Arabic, has been preserved in the mountainous regions. Many of the festivals and more colorful aspects of Morocco are Berber in origin.
- *Religious Beliefs:* The official religion of Morocco is Islam. Morocco Muslims belong to the Malekite creed, one of the four orthodox creeds of Islam. The religion is based on the Koran as dictated by Allah to the prophet, Mohammed and his Hadith (The Prophet's teachings). The word "Islam" means "Submission to Allah." Moslems are monotheistic, professing that "There is no God other than Allah, and Mohammed is his prophet." Muslims must fulfill four obligations in life: prayer, fasting, alms giving, and pilgrimage.
- *Fez:* Besides being the name of the oldest city in Morocco, fez (or fes) is also the name of the caps worn by Moroccans. Stories have it that in the early eighteenth century, Muslim invaders overran the city of Fez, shouting: "There is no God but Allah, and Muhammad is his prophet." Whoever did not subscribe to the Islamic faith was killed (thus, the symbol of Prophet Mohammed holding the Koran in one hand and a sword in the other).

  In the heat of this reported religious zealousness, the streets literally ran red with the blood of the "infidels." The Muslim invaders dipped their caps in the blood of the infidels as a testimony to Allah. These blood-soaked caps eventually became known as fezzes and were considered a badge of honor for those who proselytize the Islamic faith upon the unbelieving.
- *Medina:* the old non-European part of a city where a more traditional way of life may take place.
- *Market (Soulk):* In a soulk, tents are erected early in the morning. Soon they are full of brightly colored clothes, embroidered gowns, leather goods, slippers, teas, spices, copperware, and crafts. The soulk is busy all day as products are bought and sold or bartered, with lots of haggling and bargaining. The soulk takes on the characteristic of a village bazaar where storytellers, fortunetellers, acrobats, and food hawkers provide an exotic ambience.

Camel Notes

The Arabian camel has just one hump and is native to North Africa, India, and the Near East. The Bactrian camel has two humps and is found in the highlands of central Asia. The Arabian camel is longer-legged than the Bactrian, its coat is shorter, it is taller (about 7 feet, or 2 meters) overall though more lightly built, and its colors range from white to black. The Bactrian camel is usually brown and has a thick, shaggy coat in winter.

Do camels really store water in their humps? No, their humps store fat, which acts as an energy reserve for the animal. Camels can go for several days without drinking water, but then they'll regain lost body weight by drinking as much as 25 gallons of water at once, in just minutes. They can live on meagre rations such as dried grasses and thorny plants.

A camel's feet, soft and wide with two spreading toes, are specially adapted for travel on sand or snow. Its eyes get extra protection from two rows of eyelashes, it can close its nostrils, and its ear openings are protected by lots of hairs. When a camel kneels, its chest and knees have horny pads that support it. It's an ideal animal for desert travel.

Camels are used for transporting people and supplies; they are also valued for their milk, meat, wool, and hides. When they are properly trained, they are docile, but if they become annoyed, they'll spit or bite or kick.

Bibliography

Czernecki, Stefan, *Zorah's Magic Carpet*, Hyperion Press (Winnipeg, Canada), 1995. Zorah lives with her husband near Fez, Morocco. She longs to see faraway places, but Akhmed thinks she's foolish. She makes a beautiful carpet from the wool of a talking sheep, and it takes her to the Ukraine, India, and China. Each intricate illustration is surrounded by a border of Moroccan patterns. Grades 1+.

Haskins, Jim, *Count Your Way Through the Arab World*, Carolrhoda Books (Minneapolis), 1987. Morocco is an Arab state in terms of language, religions, and culture. Your students will learn from this book that Muslims must bow in prayer five times a day, the six reasons why the camel is so important, eight different ways to say "cousin," and more. Grades 1+.

Hermes, Jules, *The Children of Morocco*, Carolrhoda Books (Minneapolis), 1995. Photographs and stories about the daily lives of many Moroccan children and their families.

Hintz, Martin, *Enchantment of the World: Morocco*, Childrens Press (Chicago), 1985. Learn the history of Morocco, visit the imperial cities (including Fez), and see the trade and industry that is important to the nation. Well illustrated. Grade 4+.

Lawton, Clive A., *Celebrating Islam: The Customs, Culture, and Religion of Muslims Around the World*, Young Library (Corsham, England), 1995. The illustrations are great, and a map shows locations of Muslim populations. The book contains "Find out more about..." sections scattered throughout, with information on Ramadan, Arabic writing, making pita bread, etc. Grade 4+.

Lewin, Ted, *Market!*, Lothrop, Lee & Shepard Books, (New York), 1996. Markets around the world, including the souks of Morocco.

Mernissi, Fatima, *Dreams of Trespass: Tales of a Harem Gilrhood*, Addison-Wesley (Reading, Massachusetts), 1994. Adolescent girls may enjoy this story by a woman born into a traditional household in Fez in 1940.

Moktefi, Mokhtar, *The Arabs in the Golden Age*, Millbrook Press (Brookfield, Connecticut), 1992. The history of the Arabs, how they extended their empire, what life was like at a time when their creativity was at its zenith.

Morocco, Alfred A. Knopf (New York), 1994. This is a wonderful resource on Morocco! Each page is studded with photographs and illustrations, and 18 pages are devoted to the city of Fez.

Seward, Pat, *Cultures of the World: Morocco*, Marshall Cavendish (New York), 1995. This book, aimed at ages 8 to 12, contains pictures on every page. It is informative and covers a multitude of topics: history, geography, government, economy, the people, lifestyle, religion, language, arts, leisure, festivals, and even recipes!

Stewart, Judy, *A Family in Morocco*, Lerner Publications (New York), 1986. Part of the "Families the World Over" series.

Zeghidour, Slimane, *I Want to Talk to God*, Moonlight Publishing (London), 1993. An exquisitely illustrated story from Islam that your youngest students will enjoy listening to. Older students will have a better appreciation for the side notes and explanations in the margins. The book ends with information about Islam. Grades 1+.

Wall 2 Bonampak Murals: A Manifestation of Maya Civilization

Pre-Reading Warm-Up

1. Class Discussion on the Ethics of Archaeology

"The children that visit the murals today can't see the pictures very well because the ancient paint is chipping off the walls."

In 1946, a professional photographer discovered the three rooms of Maya paintings at Bonampak, Chiapas, Mexico. The world then became aware of the finest Post-Classic Maya wall paintings. The ruins of Bonampak became a popular site for archaeologists, historians, students of antiquities, and curious sightseers. As the dense undergrowth and rainforest surrounding the ruins were cleared, the structure where the ancient murals were housed was suddenly exposed to a hot and dry climate after over a thousand years of being hidden in the cool, damp jungle. The murals began to dry out and flake off the walls.

Discuss with your class the entire issue of archaeological excavation as opposed to natural preservation of a historic site. Pose the question: Once an ancient Maya site is exposed, how do we protect it from nature and greedy looters?

Invite an archaeologist from your local college, university, or community to speak on the ethics of archaeological excavations.

Language Arts

2. Letter Writing

The following addresses are provided for your students to write for information about the latest developments in archaeological excavations of Maya sites. The literature and color pictures they will receive will be exciting for them. They can use the materials to construct a Maya mural of their own.

In Mexico

Instituto Nacional de Anthropologia
    e Historia de Mexico
Moneda 16 Centro, 06060
Mexico D.F.
Ph. (5) 522-5886

Centro Regional del Instituto Nacional de
    Anthropologia e Historia de Mexico
Calzada de los Hombres Ilustres
    s/n. Tuxtla Gutierrez,
Chiapas
Mexico
Ph. (961) 3-4501, 2-0459; Fax 3-4454

Secretaria de Turismo de Mexico (SECTUR)
Avda Presidente Masarik 172, 8,
11587 Mexico, D.F.
Ph. (5) 250-8228; Fax (5) 250-4406

In the USA	In Canada
Embassy of the United Mexican States	Embassy of the United Mexican States
1911 Pennsylvania Avenue NW	45 O'Connor Street, Suite 1500
Washington, DC 20006	Ottawa, Ontario
USA	Canada, K1P 1A4
Ph. (202) 728-1600; Fax (202) 234-7739	Ph. (613) 133-8989; Fax (613) 235-9123

3. Creative Writing: Historic Fiction

It remains a mystery why the Maya left Bonampak, after they had painstakingly documented the historic events of their lives. Some scientists suggested that war or adverse environmental factors had caused the Maya to abandon Bonampak.

Assign your students to write a fictional story about what might have happened in the last days, weeks, or months before the Maya left Bonampak. Some students could choose the famine theory, others could choose the war theory; still others could make up their own reasons for the Maya's departure.

4. "Ode of an Archaeologist"

Assign your students to imagine themselves as a well-known archaeologist. Ask them to describe their training, goals, sponsorship, glories of discoveries, and frustrations. Invite them to select any literary genre: poetry, journal, story, essay, or drama.

Social Studies

5. Social Participation: Reaching Out to The Maya of Today

The Maya today number about six million people, many of whom live in Mexico. Modernization and intermarriage between the indigenous population and Spanish immigrants make it necessary for modern-day Maya to work hard to preserve their culture and identity.

Involve your school in meeting one of the learning outcomes of the discipline of social studies—social participation. With the prior approval of your school administrator, organize a fund-raiser to assist in raising the standard of living of the Maya. The MayaQuest invites you and your school to take part in such a project. (See Activity #17 for Internet Resources.)

Your school can help install a water purifying system in a school in the Maya region. Waterborne diseases such as cholera and dysentery are some of the biggest killers in Central America. Every donation of $25 from your school will be matched by MayaQuest'96 expedition sponsor PentaPure, maker of water purifying systems, and the funds raised will go towards the installation of a water purifying system in a school.

Here's how it works: Raise $25 through sales of Native "O" MayaQuest T-shirts or sweatshirts or design a fund-raising campaign of your own. For details call: 1-800-919-MAYA and request a MayaQuest water project form.

6. Geography of the Americas: The Maya Empire

The Maya Empire, like the Roman Empire, occupied a wide geographic area as evidenced by the remains of their civilization in the following regions of Meso-and-South America:

In Mexico: Chichen Itza, Dzilbilchaltun, Edzna, Hochob, Kabah, Labna, Sayil, Xpuhil, and Uxmal in the Yucatan Penninsula; Palenque, Tonina, Yaxchilan, and Bonampak in Chiapas; Cholula, 80 miles east of Mexico City; Laventa and Comalcalco in Tabasco; Tulum and Coba in Quintana; and Edzna and Calakmul in Campeche.

In Guatemala: Tikal, Piedras Negras, Ceibal, and Quirigua.

In Belize: Lamanal, Caracol, and Xunantunich.

In Honduras: Copan.

In El Salvado: Joya de Ceren

Provide your students with a big wall map of the Americas. Ask your students to locate and place colored pins on the map, using the list above, where historic sites of Maya civilization remain today. "The Ancient Maya World, A Wall Map" from *National Geographic*, could assist with this activity (see the bibliography at the end of this chapter).

7. History: A Study of Pre-Columbian Art

The paintings found in the three rooms at Bonampak are quintessential of Maya art of the Post-Classic period. The paintings depict wars, enslavement, victory celebrations with human sacrifices, and the succession of an heir to the throne.

For 3,000 years before the European discovery and colonization of the Western Hemisphere, the indigenous peoples of Central and South America developed civilizations that rivaled the artistic and intellectual accomplishments of ancient China, India, Mesopotamia, and the Mediterranean world.

Arrange to take your class to visit your local public library. Lead the students in researching the Post-Classic period of Maya art. References such as Mary Ellen Miller's authoritative and scholarly treatment of *The Murals of Bonampak* (please refer to the bibliography at the end of this chapter) should be a help.

As an extension activity, lead your class in identifying European art of about the same era as the Bonampak period in history. Compare and contrast samples of European art with those found at Bonampak and other parts of the Maya Empire.

8. Investigative History

Explore with your class the possible causes of the decline of the Maya. Discuss the conjectured factors which precipitated the downfall. What can we learn from this? Compare and contrast the decline of the Maya with that of the Roman Empire, Mesopotamia, Napoleon Bonaparte, and the Third Reich.

Science

9. Make a Plaster Cast

Plaster casts are often used in archaeology to record found evidence that would be destroyed if moved. Using animal or plant prints in the mud, or making your own depressions in modelling clay, pour plaster of Paris (reconstituted if dry) into the molds. Leave to dry (anywhere from a few minutes to an hour, depending on the type of plaster used); lift from the mud or separate from the clay, and you have a plaster cast showing the shape, texture and size of the object that made the imprint. Each student can make his/her own plaster cast.

10. Archaeological Dig:

As an extension learning activity, with the prior approval of your school administrator, bury "artifacts" (these could be common, everyday items from a garage sale or even from the garbage—the idea is the dig, not what is found) in the school yard (a sand pit, if you have one, is an ideal place). Lead your students in re-creating an archaeological dig. Be as scientific with your dig as possible. Steps used by archaeologists as they work are:

    A) Prospecting for sites with a magnetometer;

    B) Mapping the site;

    C) Creating a grid pattern on site (allows identification of exact location of objects found and matches the grid on the map);

    D) Excavations;

    E) Photographing the find;

    F) Recording the findings with pen and paper;

G) Sweeping;

H) Preserving the site.

If you choose to use a grid for your archaeological dig, begin by placing one long stake at each corner of your dig site. Connect the stakes by string into a rectangular shape. The string should be high enough off the ground that your budding archaeologists can lie under the string and work. Now attach more string to the perimeter to create a grid (each square can be the size you wish, but two feet square is a good size).

A) Each student should be assigned a grid space to work in;

B) Start by searching the grass or surface for artifacts. Anything found should be placed in plastic bags and labelled "found in grass," along with the grid identification;

C) Cut the turf in small squares as you search (turf is to be replaced when the dig is finished);

D) Draw what you see (a top plan)—large rocks, wood, artifacts etc. (This is done daily on a real archaeological site as the first activity of the day.)

E) Dig slowly using small trowels and brushes. As an object is unearthed, demonstrate how it must not be yanked out of the ground, but rather the soil or sand around it must be cleared away until it can be lifted out gently. The brush can be used to gently remove residue from the ground since the trowel is too rough for that purpose.

F) Enjoy!

See the bibliography for more information on archaeology and how it is done.

Mathematics

11. Applying Knowledge: An Estimation Activity

The frijoles recipe below can double as a mathematics estimation activity. Have the students measure the volume and weight of the beans before adding the water. Each student can predict what volume and weight the beans will be in the morning. Record their individual estimates.

In the morning drain the water and re-measure the volume and weight of the beans. Ask students to observe and measure how much the beans increased (the increase should be about 300% in volume). Why? Whose prediction came closest?

Arts and Crafts

12. Wall Paintings

With the help of your school teacher-librarian, an art educator in your local faculty of fine art, or a community member, present a lesson on famous artwork that has been painted on walls around the world. Arrange with your guests to show photographs or slides of those mural paintings to your class. Discuss how these wall paintings are being preserved.

For excellent photographic images of the mural paintings of the Maya at Bonampak, obtain a copy of Mary Ellen Miller's book, *The Murals of Bonampak*, from your local public library. Please refer to the bibliography of this chapter for bibliographical information on this reference book.

13. Creative Thinking Through Simulation

Encourage your students to create either an ancient, present, or a future culture. Ask them to identify as many components (such as music, language, religion, social structure, education, art, etc.) of that culture as they can. As an arts-and-crafts activity, ask your students to manufacture artifacts of their culture. Set aside a day for presentation and a show-and-tell display of their products in their home-spun "museum of ancient history."

14. Guest Speaker on Art Education

Have students research other paintings, both ancient and modern, that are hard to see due to chipping paint. Example are the cave paintings found in Lascaux Cave in France, the aboriginal art found in the cave walls of Australia (please refer to *Talking Walls* and *Talking Walls Teacher's Guide*, published by Tilbury House, Publishers, 1992), and the fresco paintings by the famous Italian artist, Michaelangelo, on the ceiling of the Sistine Chapel in St. Peter's Basilica in Rome.

Invite an art conservationist from your local art museum to speak to your class about techniques of art preservation. Discover how famous works of art have been restored with today's techniques and technology

15. Fresco Painting

"Fresco painting was practiced. Particularly fine examples have been found at Bonampak, Palenque, and Tikal." (Robert I. Loescher, "Pre-Columbian Art and Architecture," Microsoft (R) Encarta, 1993.)

Explore with your class the popularity and technique of fresco painting in the Renaissance period in Europe.

Food Experience

16. Recipe:

Frijoles

Beans are an important part of the Mexican diet, especially among the many who are too poor to afford meat.

Ingredients:
1 pound pinto beans
6 cups water
1/2 teaspoon ground cuminseed (optional)
2 garlic cloves (optional)
1 teaspoon salt
2 tablespoons bacon fat, lard, or margarine

Method:
1. Wash beans well.
2. Place beans in large saucepan and cover with the water. Let the beans soak, covered, overnight.
3. Add remaining ingredients.
4. Bring to a boil.
5. Reduce heat and simmer over very low heat for 1-1/2 hours.
6. Drain and serve.

Note: Frijoles may be eaten as is, served in taco shells with all the fixings, or mashed and fried in a generous amount of fat (Frijoles Fritos) and served with grated cheese.

Internet Resources

17. Maya Quest

The Minnesota Educational Computing Consortium (MECC), a non-profit computer education organization, has been sponsoring, since 1995, a team of five cycling explorers who meet with on-site archaeologists at various Maya ruins in Central and South America. They send back electronic reports to classrooms around the world. These classrooms, with a total of over one million students, help to lead the expedition by way of the Internet.
URL: *http://www/mecc.com/MAYA/MQll.html*

This Internet site is rich with usable material and is a great place to send your students for research. At the time of writing, the site is called "MayaQuest '96." However, since this project has been so successful, it seems reasonable that it will continue. If the URL does not work in subsequent years, type "MayaQuest" in a search engine of your Internet provider (Netscape, etc.), and you should find it with no problem. Further, you may wish to save this unit for when the next expedition takes place, so that your students can participate with the travellers and archaeologists. In 1996, the expedition began at the beginning of March and lasted six weeks. Following is some of what is offered on this site:

- News of the team while they are on tour, with photos
- Detailed journalling, aimed at students, about the Maya, the Maya places visited. and the team's experiences (a good example, if nothing else, of journalling, but very rich in colorful commentary)
- Collection of photo mysteries to solve through research (solutions given)
- Photos, audio clips, video clips
- Map of the team's trip
- Question of the week, e.g., "Come up with a list of the nine insights that the Maya possessed (sources of information are given); or "If it took 24 man hours to cut one brick and it took 10 men 17 minutes to move the brick, and Temple I took 150,000 bricks to build, how many man hours did it take?"
- Profiles of present-day Maya kids (and their pictures) living in the Maya regions.
- Questions ("tons" of them) from students, answered by a field of 30 archaeologists with topics ranging from sacrifice, warfare, and Maya beauty, to snakes, gold, and divorce.
- E-mail excerpts from classes to the Quest team
- Teacher to Teacher Center: "created for teachers to exchange ideas and share lesson plans with teachers all over the world about MayaQuest...." If you wish, you may go directly to:

URL: *http://www.ties.k12.mn.us/~mayatch/mq96/index.html*

It's an excellent resource, and you will find here:

- Lesson plans
- Classroom activities
- Teacher resources
- Teacher to teacher discussion archives
- Theme-based school projects
- Etc.
- Much more.

If you have questions or comments about the MayaQuest Web site, send e-mail to: *mayaquest-webmaster@list.mecc.com.*

18. Science Museum of Minnesota—Maya Adventure

The Science Museum of Minnesota presents this kid-friendly World Wide Web site. To access, go to:
URL: *http://www.sci.mus.mn.us/sln/ma/*

- Colored photos of Maya sites (many)
- Interesting details about individual Maya topics
- Information and commentary about such topics as
  - textile art (illustrations)
  - clothing (illustrations)
  - cenotes
- Maps
- Diagrams
- Architecture
- Activities (make your own cenote)
- Reproducible puzzle page.

At the time of writing, the site is not as fully developed as, hopefully, it will become. Though it has much potential, and what is there is excellent, it is still a little barren (except for the multitude of photos).

E-mail address: *mpetrich@sci.mus.mn.us*

19. Mystery of the Maya with Canadian Museum of Civilization

The Canadian Museum of Civilization in Hull, Quebec, offers an educational, kid-friendly, World Wide Web site on the *Mystery of the Maya*. You can access this Web site through:

URL: *http://www.cmcc.muse.digital.ca/membrs/civiliz/maya/mminteng.html*

You will need to register to use this site (no charge). To do so, look amongst the small print further down the opening page and click on "register." Find the "Information Desk," and scroll down to "Mystery of the Maya" and click on the title, OR, go to "Site Search" and type in "Maya." You will find here:

Maya Civilization

- Peoples, geography, and languages
- Cities of the ancient Maya
- Maya Society
- Cosmology and religion
- Writing and hieroglyphics
- Mathematics
- Maya calendar
- Astronomy
- Maya today
- Civilization time line
- Glossary
- Seven slide shows of photos (these are great!)

Exhibits of the Maya:

(Visit the museum plaza where six exhibits are on display.) For each exhibit there are color photographs, commentary, and links to even more information. In this "virtual tour" you can see:

The Temple Pyramid: with a chance to explore the interior and look at

Hieroglyphs from the Temple of the Inscriptions at Palinque;

The discovery of Pacal's tomb (commentary on the process of discovery);

Pacal's tomb (see the beauty of the tomb and learn who this man was); Classic Maya cities (what they must have looked like before they fell into ruin).

Sculptures of

Red Jaguar Throne from Chichen Itza (photos from different views);

Toltec warrior (replica of a stone column at Tula, Mexico); Chac-Mool (one example of the fourteen Chac-Mool sculptures at Chichen Itza);

Two-headed serpent (a symbol of the Aztec rain god).

Organic Garden: How and what did the Maya farm? The museum garden grows some of each.

Canatina La Palapas: Here food is prepared and shared with visitors. What foods did the Maya prepare? Click on "Maya Cuisine" for more information.

Boutique Maya: One mark of civilization is the ability to rise above subsistence living and engage in trade. What products did the Maya market? What was their currency? Want to purchase some useful classroom material? Order through the cyberboutique or click on the e-mail address for further ordering information.

IMAX Film (also see "Community Resources" below)
- A more complete synopsis of the film:
- Production notes (worthwhile checking out if you see the film).

People of the Jaguar
- Photos of artifacts with excellent commentary
- Link to MayaQuest Study Guide where you can find activities and discussion questions based on the Maya relationship with the jaguar.
http://mayaquest.mecc.com/MQ.Resources-StudyGuide.html

Links to other Maya sites:
Maya Quest
Maya Adventure
Maya Civilization—Past and Present
Maya
Native Web's Maya Page
Maya Astronomy Page
Astrology of the Ancient Maya
Many others

Community Resources

20. An IMAX Motion Picture: "The Mystery of the Maya"

Filmed on location at numerous sacred sites throughout the Maya regions, *The Mystery of the Maya* is the first giant-screen motion picture, filmed in the Canadian-designed IMAX technology, to explore the culture, science, and history of the Maya. A joint Canadian-Mexican venture, the film was co-produced by the National Film Board of Canada, the Instituto Mexicano de Cinematografia, and the Canadian Museum of Civilization.

In the film, one re-enactment recounts the amazing discovery of the spectacular Bonampak murals by photographer Giles Healey, in 1946.

After you have introduced to your class the glories of the Maya, check to see if you have an IMAX theatre nearby and plan an excursion to view this extraordinary film. IMAX and OMNIMAX are high-fidelity motion picture systems that use state-of-the-art technology to create images of unsurpassed clarity and impact on a giant screen 60 feet by 80 feet. There are 51 theatres in the U.S., 10 in Canada, and 6 in Mexico. These theaters often provide special discounts for school groups. For more information, call 416-960-8509 or fax 416-960-8596.

Teacher's Notes

Teacher Training Seminar: This is an all-day kick-off event, hosted by the Minnesota Science Museum whenever a MayaQuest expedition is about to begin. It offers workshops on technology, archaeology, and Maya culture. Call 1-800-221-9444.

MECC Software: MECC's software recreates the MayaQuest experience and interfaces with on-line programs. Runs on all Macintosh or Windows computers. To order, call 1-800-685-6322 ext. 529.

Free Electronic Field Trip: This electronic field trip was completely produced by students from Hopkins High School in Minnesota. It is available free to schools with satellite capabilities or cable access. Info: 1-612-988-4668 or e-mail: *TVLive@InforMNs.k12.mn.us*

Newton's Apple: Watch for the MayaQuest story on Newton's Apple on PBS.

Videos:

Two Worlds Touch: A Ten-Year-Old Mayan Boy's World (Environmental Media, P.O. Box 1016.

Chapel Hill, NC 27514; 800-368-3382). Teaching guide with video.

In Search of the Maya (Madera Cinevideo, 525 East Yosemite Ave., Madera, CA 93638; 800-828-8118). 1995.

The Lost Kingdom of the Maya (National Geographic Video), 1993.

Simulation Game: Maya: A Simulation of Mayan Civilization During the Seventh Century (Interaction Publishers, Box 997, Lakeside, CA 92040; 619-448-1474).

Bibliography

Adams, Richard E.W., "Archaeologists Explore Guatemala's Last City of the Maya: Rio Azul," *National Geographic*, April 1986. Rio Azul had been badly looted before the archaeologists arrived. Finding two untouched tombs on the same site enabled them to shed light on the looted areas. Adams sketches the probable history of the city, dating back to 250 B.C. and includes a map of the Maya realm and a drawing of his speculations on the appearance of Rio Azul at its zenith. The article has a wealth of information and photographs.

"The Ancient Maya World," *National Geographic*, October 1989. This wall map shows an uncountable number of officially recorded archaeological sites (the numerous red dots make the map look like it has the measles!). Also on this map is the "Epic of the Ancient Maya," a pictorial time line, and "Land of the Maya: A Traveller's Map," including roads, protected areas, museums, ruins, points of interest, etc.

"Archaeological Techniques," *Growing up with Science: The Illustrated Encyclopedia of Invention, Volume 1*, H.S. Stuttman, Inc. (Westport, Connecticut) 1984. Topics covered in this article are: excavating, preserving valuables, finding sites from the air, magnetic fields, dating methods, and underwater archaeology.

Baquedano, Elizabeth, *Eyewitness Books: Aztec, Inca, and Maya*, Stoddart (Toronto, Canada), 1993. Each page is filled with pictures of artifacts and drawings of people and the lifestyles of the period. Information on religions life, trade, food and drink, cities, sports and games, etc. Even your youngest students will appreciate the pictures.

Brouwer, Sigmund, *The Accidental Detectives: Sunrise at the Mayan Temple*. Victor Books (Wheaton, Illinois), 1992. A detective novel for ages 8-12. Ricky's six year-old brother mysteriously receives free plane tickets to Mexico and an invitation to help with the archaeological dig at Chichen Itza. Ricky, his friends, brother, and chaperone find themselves embroiled in a mystery when a Maya girl's father disappears.

Cenote of Sacrifice: Maya Treasures from the Sacred Well at Chichen Itza, Univeristy of Texas Press (Austin), 1984. Photographs on every page.

Chrisp, Peter, *Look into the Past: The Maya*, Wayland (Hove, England), 1994. Glossary and pronunciation guide, photographs of found items, and drawings with simple descriptions. Grade 3+.

Coe, Michael D., *Breaking the Maya Code*, Thames and Hudson (London), 1992. Though directed to adults, this book is full of line drawings of glyphs with accompanying translations, charts of glyphs, and even a comparison with other logographic languages.

Demarest, Arthur A., "The Violent Saga of a Maya Kingdom," *National Geographic*, February 1993. In the Petexbatun region of Guatemala, archaeologists are finding clues to the fate of Maya civilization. Reconstructive drawings of settlements and city-states are part of this excellent article.

Fash, William, *Scribes, Warriors, and Kings: The City of Copan and the Ancient Maya*, Thames and Hudson (London), 1991. This is a firsthand account of archaeological work in Copan, one of the great cities of the Classic Maya. The plentiful photographs and drawings will make it interesting for intermediate students.

Fasquelle, Ricardo Agurcia and William L. Fash Jr., "Copan: A Royal Maya Tomb Discovered," *National Geographic*, October 1989. The archaeologists' focus was on the commoners of the city of Copan. Instead they found the tomb of a nobleman. Follow the team as they wrestle with who this might be.

Fasquelle, Ricardo Agurcia and William Fash Jr., "Maya Artistry Unearthed," *National Geographic*, September 1991. In Copan, a smaller temple is found, intentionally preserved by the Maya, inside a larger temple pyramid. The relics are exquisite.

Garrett, Wilber, "La Ruta May," *National Geographic*, October 1989. Five nations have collaborated to create a 1,500-mile (2,400-km) route connecting Maya sites. Join the author as he travels this road, and see fantastic pictures of ruins, wildlife, and people.

Gifford, Douglas, *Warriors, Gods, and Spirits from Central and South American Mythology*, Peter Bedrick Books (New York), 1983. Pages 30–51 contain stories from Maya mythology, which you can read or retell even to the youngest students or allow older students to read themselves. Grade 5+.

Graham, Ian, "Looters Rob Graves and History," *National Geographic*, April 1986. Against a backdrop of incredibly clear hieroglyphic inscriptions left behind in Tomb 1 at Rio Asul, Graham looks at the history of archaelogical looting and the destruction and problems it causes.

Hammond, Norman, "Unearthing the Oldest Known Maya," *National Geographic*, July 1982. The ruins of Cuello, Belize, indicate the Maya culture existed 4,000 years ago!

La Fay, Howard, "The Maya: Children of Time" *National Geographic*, December 1975. Modern and ancient Maya are compared.

Lemonick, Michael D., "Secrets of the Maya," *Time* (Canada) magazine, August 9, 1993. Beginning with a tale of Maya ritual, Lemonick discusses theories of the Maya downfall, life in a typical family, and the translation of glyphs. Photographs of ruins, artwork, and archaeologists at their job are included.

Lost Civilizations: The Magnificent Maya, Time-Life Books (Alexandria, Virginia), 1993. A very readable book for older students. Filled with full-page color photographs—a delightful addition to the classroom.

Matheney, Ray T., "An Early Maya Metropolis Uncovered: El Mirador," *National Geographic*, September 1987. They look like hills but are really ancient Maya buildings uncharted by archaeologists until 1962. Paintings by T.W. Rutledge add life to this complex city and enable the reader to imagine what civilized life was like there. Included is a map of Maya territory and a city blueprint.

McIntosh, Jane, *Eyewitness Books: Archaeology*, Stoddart (Toronto), 1994. As expected with this series, this book is crammed full of color photographs, illustrations, and drawings with snippets of information filling in the empty spaces. A student can open the book anywhere and instantly learn a little or a lot. Find here an underground cutaway, the process of restoration, dating, preservation, and more. Ages six and up (but don't be fooled; there is a lot here that most teachers don't know).

Miller, Mary Ellen, "Maya Masterpiece Revealed at Bonampak," *National Geographic*, February 1995. A "must read" for all teachers and classes, this article contains wonderful detail of the murals. Miller shows how the murals' beauty is being restored through computer reconstruction.

Miller, Mary Ellen, *The Murals of Bonampak*, Princeton University Press (Princeton), 1986. The detail of Miller's scholarly work is beyond the scope of most classrooms. However, the drawing and photographs are worth consideration even for grade 1, and the resourceful teacher could develop extra activities from the book, such as attempting to mimic and wear the costumes of the murals from Miller's detailed descriptions.

Odijk, Pamela, *The Mayas*, Silver Burdett Press (Englewood Cliffs, New Jersey), 1990. Although aimed at children, the text is perhaps too scholarly for young students. Excellent photographs. Grade 5+.

Pettersen, Carmen L., *The Maya of Guatemala: Their Life and Dress*, Ixchel Museum (Guatemala City), 1976. The present-day Maya of Guatemala love color, which is clearly demonstrated by the clothes they wear. The author, an accomplished artist who lives among the Maya of Guatemala, has painted 60 portraits of the Maya in costume. The book is bilingual (English and Spanish) and easy to read for intermediate students.

"Plaster Casts," *Growing up with Science: The Illustrated Encyclopedia of Invention, Volume 25*, H.S. Stuttman, Inc (Westport, Connecticut), 1984. Use plaster of paris to make casts of shells, coins etc.

Porell, Bruce, *Digging the Past: Archaeology in your own Backyard*, Addison-Wesley (Reading, Massachusetts), 1979. Very readable for grades 4 and up, even grade 1 can benefit from this book with a little help from the teacher. The author interacts with the reader, making suggestions for activities students can do with great ease. The book is full of wonderful ideas for games and activities, and contains lots of information on archaeology.

"Restoration," *Growing up with Science: The Illustrated Encyclopedia of Invention, Volume 14*, H.S. Stuttman, Inc. (Westport, Connecticut), 1984. An essential part of an archaeologist's task is to restore the discovered artifacts to their past glory. This article shows how it's done.

Roberts, David, "The Decipherment of Ancient Maya," *Atlantic Monthly* September 1991. It has taken a long time for archaeologists to understand the glyphs found in Maya ruins. Here is a history of the search for comprehension, along with some translated glyphs. If you have access to this magazine, it might be fun to try and find these same glyphs in photographs elsewhere and see if you and the students can make any meaning from them. (One of the foremost current glyph experts wrote his first scholarly paper on the subject when he was only twelve years old!)

Schele, Linda and David Freidel, *A Forest of Kings: The Untold Story of the Ancient Maya*, William Morrow and Company (New York), 1990. Nearly every page has line drawings of glyphs, stellas, etc. Written for adults, but intermediate students will enjoy this.

Stuart, George E., "City of Kings and Commoners: Copan," *National Geographic*, October 1989. Discovered in 1839 and bought for $50 from a local farmer, Copan has gradually revealed its secrets of the Maya world. Photographs of discoveries and paintings of active life in the city are included.

Stuart, George E., "Maya Art Treasures Discovered in Cave," *National Geographic*, August 1981. Naj Tunich, a cave in the Peten region of Guatemala, is full of inscriptions and glyphs. Fifteen-year-old glyph expert David Stuart, accompanies his father and others on an exploration of this cave.

Stuart, George, "Maya Heartland Under Siege," *National Geographic*, November 1992. The Peten region in Northern Guatemala is under attack by axe and chainsaw wielders hoping to gain more land for growing crops. In the process they are destroying the forest and its treasures of wildlife, and exposing archaeological sites to looters, and erasing whole chapters of human and natural history.

Stuart, Georg E., "The Maya: Riddle of the Glyphs," *National Geographic*, December 1975. Glyphs, once thought to be inscriptions solely about the gods, are discovered to have much wider meaning. Also, Maya writing is found to be not phonetic, like European languages, but pictorial like Chinese, with each glyph having an intrinsic meaning. A four-page reproduction of glyphs and paintings is translated for us by the author.

Stuart, George, "Mural Mysteries of the Ancient Cacaxtla," *National Geographic*, September 1992. The Cacaxtla city lies more than 300 miles outside of the known Maya region, yet it bears a striking resemblance to other Maya cities. Why?

Science and its Secrets: Archaeology, Raintree Publishers (Milwaukee), 1988. Of particular interest to students grade 8 and under are the diagrams of archaeological process, tools of the archaeologists, and information on how the archaeologists do their work.

Tickell, James and Oliver Tickell, *Travel to Landmarks: Tikal, City of the Maya*, Tauris Parke Books (London), 1991. Tikal was the greatest of the Classical Maya cities. The book is written for adults, but children will love the excellent color photographs.

Wilkerson, S. Jeffrey K., "The Usumacinta River: Troubles on a Wild Frontier," *National Geographic*, October 1985. The river travels through ancient Maya territory, but the race for development threatens both the Maya legacy and the ecological balance.

Wall 3 Tibet: A Courageous People, A Robust Land

Pre-Reading Warm-Up

1. A Study of Religions

A) Ask your students what prayer is. Write their answers on the chalkboard. If it seems appropriate in your class, invite students to share the prayers with which they are familiar.

B) Explore with your class the many ways that prayers may be said, such as chants, hymns, sacred music, group prayers, private prayers, led responses, meditations, recitations, and liturgical rituals, to mention a few.

C) Introduce the Tibetan mode of praying with the prayer wheel. (Please refer to the "Teacher's Notes" section of this chapter). Discuss the ways turning the prayer wheel is similar to or different from: i) reciting the rosary by Catholics, and ii) the placing of pieces of written prayers into the cracks of the Western Wall by the Jews in Jerusalem.

Language Arts

2. The Dalai Lama: Creative Writing

The 14th Dalai Lama was chosen when he was three years old. When he was taken from his mother, he cried. On the way to his throne in Lhasa, the capital city, he fought with his older brother; he liked mechanical toys, played games with his guards, ran down the palace hallways, watched movies, and got bored with his studies.

Let the students pretend they are each the boy chosen to be the Dalai Lama and have been taken to live in a palace away from his parents. They can write how they feel and what they experience. If you or they prefer, they could pretend to be a different child separated from his or her parents for future greatness, like Samuel in the Bible. See the bibliography at the end of this chapter for biographies of the current Dalai Lama.

3. The History of Buddhism: A Research Project

Buddhism dates back to 528 B.C., when an Indian nobleman began to teach his countrymen ways to become free from the burden of self-gratification and obsessive materialism. He taught that there exists a better state of being, called nirvana, in which human beings are free from vice and misery.

In 747 A.D., the Buddhist monk and scholar Padmasambhava, "Born of the Lotus," traveled to Tibet from northern India. There, he established the first order of monks, or lamas. In the fourth century, a Tibetan king converted to Buddhism. Throughout 1,600 years of being practiced in Tibet, Tibetan Buddhism, also known as Tantric Buddhism, took on features of Hindu and Sufi (Islamic) philosophies, mantra (inscribed prayers), and yoga.

Assign your students to research the origin, development, and characteristics of Tibetan Buddhism. The school library, public library, Internet resources, and the local Tibetan community are sources of information for this undertaking. (Please refer to a listing of resources contained in the bibliography of this chapter.)

4. Letter Writing

Amnesty International is extremely concerned about juvenile political prisoners in Tibet. Many of the Tibetan children who are being detained—the majority of whom are novice monks and nuns—have been arrested during peaceful demonstrations around temples in Lhasa. Many of these young prisoners were tried on criminal charges and sentenced to between two and six years' imprisonment.

The inhumane treatment of juvenile prisoners in Tibet by the Chinese government violates not only its own law but international human rights treaties and the UN Convention on the Rights of the Child.

Amnesty International maintains a Web site where the problems and concerns of children being detained against their will for reasons of conscience or politics is expressed more fully. Included are some children's testimonies and a listing of those who are missing or under political arrest. When you access this site, scroll down the opening page until you reach "Juvenile Prisoners of Conscience and Political Prisoners in Tibet."
URL: *http://www.amnesty.org/Asia95171895.ASA.txt*

Encourage your students to write to the Chinese diplomatic representatives and express their concerns on how children of their age are being imprisoned and ill-treated in Tibet. The following addresses are provided for this purpose.

In the U.S.	In Canada
Embassy of the People's Republic of China	Embassy of the People's Republic of China
2300 Connecticut Avenue NW,	515 St. Patrick Street,
Washington, DC 20008	Ottawa, Ontario
USA	Canada
Ph. (202) 328-2500; Fax (202) 232-7855	K1N 5H3
	Ph. (613) 789-3434; Fax (613) 789-1911

For more information on children currently detained against their will, contact:
Amnesty International,
International Secretariat,
1 Easton Street,
London WC1X 8DJ
United Kingdom
Ph. (44) (71) 413-5500; Fax (44) (71) 956-1157
E-mail: *amnestyis@gn.apc.org*

Social Studies

5. An Exercise in Empathy Development

"Many Tibetans are not able to spin prayer wheels in their own country because they have been forced to leave Tibet and now live elsewhere."

China invaded and occupied Tibet in 1949 and 1950, claiming sovereignty over Tibet. Subsequent Chinese control and violation of a treaty that promised non-interference in Tibet's internal affairs led to the 1969 national uprising. Thousands of Tibetans, including their head of state and spiritual leader, the Dalai Lama, were forced by the Chinese invaders to to leave their homeland.

During the past 46 years of Chinese occupation in Tibet, Tibet's culture has been systematically destroyed and its people brutally suppressed through executions, tortures, imprisonment, sentences to labor camps, and the deprivation of basic human rights and dignity. The practice of Tibetan Buddhism and the raising of the Tibetan national flag are strictly prohibited by the Chinese.

Hold a discussion with your class about the sense of suppression, loss, and hopelessness we would feel if our country was invaded and occupied by a hostile foreign country. How would we feel if we were prohibited to speak our language, practice our religion, honor our flag, and live the way of life we had enjoyed? This could also be a creative-writing lesson.

6. Organize a School-Wide Fund-Raising Campaign for Tibet

Support for the Tibetan School Project

The Tibetan School Project is an international effort of Tibetan exiles and Westerners in Sweden and the USA to build and operate a grade 1-6 day and boarding school in the village of Katsel, Tibet, just outside Lhasa, the capital of Tibet. This project, which began construction in 1993, represents the first time that a foreign organization has been granted permission to build a school in Tibet. The project is now servicing 150 Tibetan children with education, preservation of their culture, clothing, feeding, and basic health care.

Financial support is needed to complete the kitchen/dining hall and dispensary. Corporate/organizational sponsorships are being sought for the construction of a vocational training center, library, a greenhouse, and the purchase of an ambulance for the region.

With the support of your school administrator and P.T.A., organize with your students (or the entire school) a fund-raiser, such as read-a-thon, math-a-thon, marathon, sale-a-thon, etc., to collect donations towards supporting school children in occupied Tibet through this project.

Donations and further information can be addressed to:

The U.S. Society for School and Culture
c/o Anne Oliver
4707 Connecticut Avenue, NW #201
Washington, DC 20008
USA
E-mail address: *shiwa@aol.com*

Note: Contributions of $100 or more to the Tibetan School Project (c/o Anne Oliver) will be given a choice of either one of the two CD's, *Made in America* by Yo Yo Ma, or *Anima Mundi* by Philip Glass.

Support for Three Tibetan Refugee Relief Projects

In the fall of 1996, Pomegranate Publications is scheduled to release a book and a calendar entitled *Tibetan Voices: A Traditional Memoir.* These publications are the main feature of a fund-raising campaign initiated by the Seva Service Society. All royalties from the sale of these two publications and other funds raised will be divided between Seva and three Tibetan refugee relief projects: The Tibetan Health Education Organization, the Nuns Project, and the Delek Hospital Aid Foundation.

Of the book, *Tibetan Voices*, the exiled Dalai Lama says," I hope this book of images will create a better understanding of Tibet, its people, and their culture whose very existence today are gravely threatened." For further information, e-mail Brian Harris at: *tibvoc@helix.net*

The *Tibetan Voices* and calendar will be available (Fall, 1996) from:

Pomegranate Publications
Box 6099
Rohnert Park, CA 94927
USA
Ph. (707) 586-5500; Fax (707) 586-5518

Seva Service Society,
200 - 2678 West Broadway,
Vancouver, B.C.
Canada
V6K 2G3
Ph. (604) 733-4284; Fax (604) 733-4292

7. The Toycott

The human rights violations committed by the Chinese officials in Tibet have caused a reverberation of outrage and opened a floodgate of independent and concerted efforts toward the Tibetan cause around the world. Student organizations have sprung up to work towards Tibet independence. On February 12, 1996 the U.S. Tibet Committee and Students for a Free Tibet held a "Toycott" demonstration at the International Toy Fair in New York. The Toycott is meant to be an on-going boycott of toys made in China.

You and your students may elect to take part in this cause at any time of the year, reminding the

Chinese leadership that the international community will not buy toys and other Chinese products that help fund the Chinese government and its continued oppression and exploitation of Chinese and Tibetan citizens.

Have your students heard of other boycotts? Have they ever boycotted something to make a peaceful protest? Some boycotts that you may wish to discuss are:

A) Exxon gas, after the *Exxon Valdez* oil spill disaster;

B) Nestle, for distributing free baby formula in poor, third-world countries. This discouraged natural breastfeeding, but later the mothers could not afford to buy the formula they needed to keep their babies healthy.

C) Table grapes in the U.S., to support the union demands of farm laborers; and

D) Cosmetics that are tested on animals.

E) Can your class think of any others?

Science

8. Animal Life of Tibet

Ask your students to name the animals that live in Tibet. You could start a list in the chalkboard, ask the children do do some research, and add to the list. Allow each child to choose an Tibetan animal to study, looking at predators, prey, usefulness to man, habitat, diet, etc.

Hume's ground jays	Snow leopard
wolf	Tibetan brown bear
Blue sheep	Black-lipped pikas
Upland hawks	Saker falcons
Sand foxes	Tibetan antelope
yak	Kiangi (wild asses)
Tibetan argali sheep	Tibetan wooly hare
lynx	Tibetan gazelle

Older students can look at the interplay of animal species on the Tibetan plateau (use *National Geographic* magazine listed in the bibliography as a reference).

9. The Himalayas

The Himalayan Mountain Range speaks of grandeur barely guessed at by us mere mortals who must be content with photographs of a place we'll never see. But even in this seemingly untouched heaven on earth, all is not Eden. Nepal alone sees nearly a million visitors a year who leave their trash and litter on the land. The poverty-ridden residents are helping to denude the mountains of their forests. Tibet is in great need of lumber to meet the needs of a growing population in the cities, and so more forests are cut.

Assign your students the task of examining/researching the ecological system of the Himalayas. Besides height and breadth, what makes this region unique? Is the threat to the ecosystem serious? What can be done to balance the needs of nature with the needs of man?

Mathematics

10. Multiples

If a prayer wheel holds one mantra, turning the wheel once is the same as praying once. Turning the wheel ten times, is the same as praying ten times. How many prayers are made if the wheel holds ten mantras and is spun four times?

Create a series of questions, based on the needs of your students, that follow this thread of thought. Those just learning multiplication can solve problems of one mantra in a wheel, if I turn it X number of times, how many prayers have been made? This can be extended to three mantras turned four times etc.

11. Exponents

The previous activity can be extended for those learning exponential notation, eg.: If a large wheel holds 1,000,000 mantras and is turned 10 times (100 times, 37 times, whatever), how many prayers have been made? Write your answer in exponential notation.

Art and Crafts

12. National Flag: The Spirit of a Nation

In occupied Tibet and elsewhere in China, it is prohibited to display or fly the Tibetan national flag, with the threat of imprisonment, reprisals, torture, and death as punishments. The following activities would help your students not only appreciate what our own national flag stands for, but also support the Tibetan cause in its peaceful struggle for independence from its colonizer China.

A) You could start by asking your students to make their own flags or a classroom or school flag. Provide your class with art paper of appropriate colors, pairs of scissors, and glue sticks.

B) Help your class explore the meaning our national flag design. Then ask them to construct a measured-to-scale national flag.

C) Ask your students to look up the meaning of the Tibetan national flag. Ask them to construct the Tibetan flag.

D) In response to the call of Tibet supporters around the world, hang your national flag alongside the Tibetan flag in your classroom or in the school hallway.

Food Experience

13. Recipes

In the high mountains of Tibet, where agriculture is limited, the yak is a primary source of food and provides milk (for cheese and yogurt) and meat. Near Tibet's border with China, there is more variety in the diet and vegetables and grains are much more available. *Moh-Moh*—steamed, stuffed dumplings— are probably the national favorite in Tibet and are usually served with a clear meat soup.

Moh-Moh

Ingredients:

Meat Filling

1 lb lamb, beef, or both	2 tsp. water
4 cloves minced garlic	15 drops Tabasco
1 tsp. minced fresh ginger	2 cups minced spinach
2 Tbsp. minced fresh cilantro	
4 Tbsp tamari	

Dumpling Dough
4 cups unbleached flour
1-1/3 cups water

Method:

1. Chop the meat into fine pieces; you could use ground meat, instead.
2. Put all of the ingredients for the meat filling in a bowl, and mix well.
3. To make the dumpling dough, stir the water into the flour in a large bowl until it forms a ball and you can knead it. Knead for a minute, then transfer the dough to a floured breadboard and knead it for two minutes longer. Cut the dough in half, and shape each half into a log shape, about a foot long, and cut it into inch-wide pieces. You should have about 24 pieces.
4. Roll each piece into a ball between the palms of your hand and then flatten it on a floured breadboard so that it is about 2-1/2 inches in diameter. Take a rolling pin and press down on the edges, rolling towards the center with less pressure so that the middle stays thicker.
5. Holding the circle of dough in one hand, place two heaping tablespoons of filling in the center, and

start to bring the edge up to the center, pinching the dough together, stretching it over the filling, and turning your hand to pleat the dough as you work your way around the top of the dumpling, pinching it to seal it.

6. Please the moh-moh on a well-greased steamer rack and steam them over boiling water for 15–20 minutes.

7. If you don't have a steamer, you can make one using a large covered pot, a few old tuna cans, and a pie tin with holes in the bottom. Grease the pie tin and place the moh-moh on the surface. Put the tuna cans in the bottom of the pot and fill the pot with water just two-thirds of the way up the sides of the tuna cans. Place the pie tin on top of the cans, so it sits just above the water, bring the water to a fast boil, cover, and steam.

Internet Resources

14. Homepage of Tibet

Many of the Internet sites that feature Tibet are heavily into political action. This one is not. It is sponsored by the Tibet Study Association and can be accessed with this address:
URL: *http://omni.cc.purdue.edu/~wtv/tibet/welcome.html*

Here you will find:
• Maps of the country and region;
• Tibetan history;
• Photos;
• A quick written tour of the country and its culture (with links to more photos and commentary);
• Information about Tibetan Buddhism.

15. Tour the Himalayas

The Shangri La homepage focuses on the Himalayan region, especially the mountains. This site specializes in wonderful photographs of the mountains. Link after link takes you to more and more photographs. This is a wonderful place for even young children, if guided by the teacher.
URL: *http://aleph0.clarku.edu/~rajs/Shangri_La.html*

16. Take a Photo Tour of Tibet

Three more sites are valuable for their photographs of Tibet. If you visit "Tibetan and Himalayan Travel," you can be linked to the other two sites. However, their URLs are included as well for ease of access.

Tibetan and Himalayan Travel:
URL: *http://www.manymedia.com/tibet/TibetTravel.html*

Tibet: A Photographic Journey (arts, people, and architecture):
URL: *http://gallery.sjsu.edu/ArtH/tibet/main.html*

Images of Tibet:
URL: *http://www-leland.stanford.edu:80/~wgs/images.html*

17. Committee of 100 for Tibet

This organization is concerned about Tibetans who are missing at the hands of the Chinese government or who are disaster victims. The stories of many of these victims are told on the following Internet site:
URL: *http://members.aol.com/Tibet100/Tibet100.html*

• Ngawang Choephel, a Tibetan who moved to India, disappeared when he revisited Tibet.
• A music teacher was arrested for photographing—location unknown.

- 200,000 nomads were affected by the 1996 blizzard—the worst in 100 years.
- The six-year-old Panchen Lama (second only to the Dalai Lama) has been missing, with his family, since November 1995. He may be under detention by Chinese authorities—whereabouts unknown.
- Others are also mentioned.
- Letter writing is encouraged, and addresses given.

> Committee of 100 for Tibet
> P.O. Box 60612
> Palo Alto, CA 94306-0612
> USA
> *E-mail: Tibet100@aol.com*

18. Students for a Free Tibet

"Students for a Free Tibet is a call to action. We must take advantage of the constitutional freedoms we have in this country, and speak out on behalf of those who are not able to do so themselves.

"...Please join us in the fight to free the Tibetan people and plateau from the brutal Chinese regime. It's not just about freeing the Tibetan people from the oppression, though—it's about bringing democracy into your own life by refusing to participate in this brutal cycle...."
URL: *http://www.cs.oberlin.edu/students/djacobs/tibet/*

The Internet site includes:

- Articles and musings about the Tibetan situation, people's stories, and experiences;
- Events sponsored by Students for a Free Tibet;
- Current news about Tibet; or you may go directly to:

URL: *http://www.iem.pw.edu.pl/~jstar/pspt/wtn.html*

- A brief history of Tibet since 1949;
- Links to other "Free Tibet" organizations.

> Students for a Free Tibet
> 241 E 32nd Street
> New York, NY 10066
> USA
> Ph. (212) 213-5010
> Fax (212) 779-9245

Teacher's Notes

Prayer Wheels

Prayer wheels are used by Tibetan Buddhists to purify themselves and the entire world of its accumulated negative karma. Inside each prayer wheel is a piece of paper on which a prayer (mantra) is inscribed many times over. Typically, the mantra is *Om Mani Padme Hum* (Tibetan pronunciation is *Om Mani Peme Hung)*, translated as "The jewel in the lotus of the heart."

Typically, a Tibetan Buddhist holds a prayer wheel in his/her right hand, and recites the mantra, Om Mani Padme Hum. When he walks around, he constantly turns the prayer wheel and recites the same prayer audibly, over and over again.

The prayer refers to the supposed hidden potential of divinity within each one of us. The six syllables of the mantra are said to purify the six negative emotions: pride, jealousy, desire, ignorance, greed, and anger. At the same time, the mantra is thought to bring about the six positive qualities of enlightenment: generosity, harmony, endurance, enthusiasm, concentration, and insight.

It is believed that if the mantra is inscribed once and placed in the prayer wheel, each rotation of the wheel accumulates the same spiritual merits as having prayed once. Turning a prayer wheel containing 100 million Om Mani Padme Hum mantras accumulates the same spiritual merits as having recited 100 million mantras. Simply touching the prayer wheel is considered to bring great purification of negative karmas.

Bibliography

Bancroft, Anne, *The Buddhist World*, MacDonald (London), 1984. See a cutaway of a Buddhist wat in Thailand. Learn about 11-year-old Tibetan boys becoming monks, the finding of the Dalai Lama, and more. Grade 5+.

Bishop, Barry C., "A Fragile Heritage: The Mighty Himalaya," *National Geographic*, November 1988. All is not well in the Himalayas. Trekkers leave litter and waste, and the forests are being cut down to provide fuel for inhabitants and trekkers alike. Bishop looks at steps being taken to halt this erosion of beauty and ecology.

Booz, Elisabeth B., *Tibet*, Passport Books (Lincolnwood, Illinois) 1986. Contains color photographs of Tibet, the people, and religious objects.

Brignoli, Frank J. and Christine Johnston Brignoli, *Lhasa: Tibet's Forbidden City*, Peter Chancellor Design Associates (Hong Kong), 1987. Enjoy the photographs of this city, her people, and their religious sites.

Garrett, Wilbur E., "Exploring Cradle Earth," *National Geographic*, November 1988. Includes a four-page fold-out panoramic view of the Himalayas with Everest in the background.

"Geology," *Growing up with Science: The Illustrated Encyclopedia of Invention, Volume 7*, H.S. Stuttman, Inc. (Westport, Connecticut), 1984. A study of mountains would not be complete without a look at the geology involved. Here is information about historical and physical geology, techniques, dating, and the history of the study of geology.

Gibb, Christopher, *People Who Have Helped the World: The Dalai Lama, The Exiled Leader of the People of Tibet and Tireless Worker for World Peace*, Gareth Stevens Children's Books (Milwaukee), 1990. He is known as the Laughing Buddha because of his humor. This biography for children tells not only about the Dalai Lama but also about the history of Tibet and the difficulties the Tibetans have had with their Chinese rulers. Lots of pictures.

Goldstein, Melvyn and Cynthia Beall, "The Remote World of Tibet's Nomads," *National Geographic*, June 1989. About half a million nomads live on the Chang Tang grasslands at about 15,000 feet. Despite appearances, at least one nomad thinks their life is easy. Although they herd sheep and goats as well, the yak is the key to the nomadic life style, providing transportation, milk, skins, and meat.

Johnson, Russell and Kerry Moran, *The Sacred Mountain of Tibet: On Pilgrimage to Kailas*, Park Street Press (Rochester, Vermont), 1989. All books should be this beautiful! Kailas is, for the Hindus, the throne of Shiva; for Buddhists it is a gigantic natural mandala. Both religions consider it the epicenter of Tantric forces. The photographs show both the magnificence of the area and the devotional reverence paid to this mountain by Tibetans.

Kohl, Larry, "Heavy Hands on the Land," *National Geographic*, November 1988. Kohl is justly concerned with man's rape of the Himalayas. However, some measures are being taken to preserve the land, such as the Everest National Park which shelters many creatures.

Levy, Patricia, *Cultures of the World: Tibet*, Marshall Cavendish (New York), 1996. "The Tibetan people have made their home in one of the most inhospitable, but also one of the msot stunning, regions of the world.... This book examines the lives of those hardy people, their ancient culture, the country's astonishing geography, and its economic and political realities today." Great pictures. Grade 5+.

Morrissey, James D., "The Forgotten Face of Everest: Conquest of the Summit," *National Geographic*, July 1984. Mount Everest straddles the border between Tibet and Nepal. This article looks at one attempt to reach the peak from the Tibetan side.

"Mountains," *Growing up with Science: The Illustrated Encyclopedia of Invention, Volume 10*, H.S. Stuttman, Inc. (Westport, Connecticut), 1984. A look at the kinds of mountains there are, how they may have been formed, why mountains have the scenery they have, and the climate, animals, and vegetation that they have. This is a simple-to-understand resource for students studying the Himalayas.

"Mountains," *The Young Children's Encyclopedia, Volume 10*, Encyclopedia Britannica Inc. (Chicago), 1977. For K-3, this entry includes the articles, How did the mountains get there?" "Who lives on mountains?" and a comic strip entitled "Let's Take a Trip Up a Mountain."

Pandell, Karen, *Learning From the Dalai Lama: Secrets of the Wheel of Time*, Dutton (New York), 1995. The text explains the personal history of the Dalai Lama.

"Scaling the Roof of the World," *Disney's Wonderful World of Knowledge Volume 7: Exploration and Discovery*, Danbury Press (Danbury, Connecticut), 1973. Mount Everest is the tallest in the world. Many have tried to scale it, but it wasn't until 1953 that anyone succeeded.

Schaller, George B., "Tibet's Remote Chang Tang: In a High and Sacred Realm," *National Geographic*, August 1993. The Chang Tang is a wilderness preserve, the highest pasture land on the Tibetan Plateau. Larger than the state of California, this preserve is the world's second largest nature preserve after Greenland National Park. A multitude of animals live here, and a detailed description of many of them can be found in this article.

Snelling, John, *Holidays and Festivals: Buddhist Festivals*, Rourke Enterprises (Vero Beach, Florida), 1987. The festivals of Tibet, Losar, Prayer Days, and others are found on pages 30–37. Grade 4+.

Snelling, John, *The Life of the Buddha*, Wayland (Hove, England), 1987. "This book retells some of the memorable episodes from the life of the Buddha, each superbly illustrated in the style of traditional Buddhist art." Grade 1+.

Snelling, John, *Religions of the World: Buddhism*, Wayland (Hove, England), 1986. Who was the Buddha? What did he teach? How to Buddhists live? What is their philosophy, their ceremonies, customs, and art? Grade 4+.

Snelling, John, *Religious Stories: Buddhist Stories*, Wayland (Hove, England), 1986. "This book retells six classic stories from the Jakata Tales of the Buddhist religion. Each is illustrated. Grade 1+.

Stewart, Whitney, *To the Lion Throne: The Story of the 14th Dalai Lama*, Snow Lion Publications (Ithaca, N.Y.), 1990. This is an easy-to-read, but informative biography of the 14th Dalai Lama.

Van Dyk, Jere, "Long Journey of the Brahmaputra," *National Geographic*, November 1988. The Brahmaputra River starts its journey in the highlands of Tibet before it meanders through eastern India and empties into the Indian Ocean via the delta in Bangladesh. Though the entire article does not focus on Tibet, enough of Tibet is discussed and revealed in photographs to make this a worthwhile read.

Washburn, Bradford, "Mount Everest: Surveying the Third Pole," *National Geographic*, November 1988. How exactly does one map such an aloof and hard-to-reach place? It's done with the combination of aerial photographs, the Columbia Space Shuttle, the Great Trigonometrical Survey of India 1849-1850, and lots of careful attention to detail (seems like a math lesson could be gotten out of this for those of you who understand trigonometry).

Wilby, Sorrel, "Nomad's Land: A Journey Through Tibet," *National Geographic*, December 1987. Wilby trekked alone and on foot 1,800 miles (2,900 km) through Tibet. Her journey yielded goat-milking lessons, temporary snow-blindness, the loss of her pack animal (on the second day), injury, and humor as well as a close, intimate look at the nomads who dominate the plateau.

Wall 4 Wat Po: Culture Carved In Stone

Pre-Reading Warm-Up

1. Culture Carved In Stone Around the World

All over the world, in times past or in the present, cultural messages are found carved in stone for the benefit of generations to come. That's why we have historical sites and buildings set aside for the preservation of the cultural history of a people.

In South Dakota, the giant heads of four U.S. presidents were carved in the granite summit of Mount Rushmore. Another gigantic rock sculpture of a plains native is near completion in the Black Hills of the same state to remind us that our history and culture are closely influenced by those of the original peoples of the Americas.

In Canada, the Parliament building in Ottawa contains a wealth of Canadian history carved in granite and marble, depicting the birth of a nation. Across the river in Hull, Quebec, is a modern structure, the Canadian Museum of Civilization, designed by a famous Metis architect, Douglas Cardinal, to resemble the natural environment of the land. The museum will always remind us that man is inescapably and closely tied to Mother Nature.

On the cliffs near the Bay of Bengal in India, larger-than-life carvings of animals were carved on the cliffface to pass on to generations to come Hindu myths and folk tales of the land. If interested, please refer to *Talking Walls* by Margy Burns Knight, published by Tilbury House, Publishers in 1992.

Invite your students and their parents to offer accounts of their visits to places where cultural messages, either in writing or in pictures, are carved in stone both at home and abroad. Collect this information and assign the class to write and publish a class anthology entitled "Culture Carved In Stone."

Students can write for more information about the Mount Rushmore National Memorial by inquiring at:

Mount Rushmore National Memorial
P.O. Box 268,
Keystone, SD 57751-0268
USA
Ph. (605) 574-2523
Fax (605) 574-2307

Language Arts

2. Letter Writing

Encourage your students to write for more information about Thailand and the Thai system of public education. The Thai authorities may provide you with school addresses to which your students can write to establish pen pals.

In Thailand	In the USA
Tourism Authority of Thailand,	Embassy of the Kingdom of Thailand,
372 Thanon Bamrung Muang,	1024 Wisconsin Avenue, N.W.,
Bangkok 10100	Washington, D.C. 20007,
Thailand	USA
Ph. (2) 226-0060; Fax (2) 226-6227	Ph. (202) 944-3600; Fax (202) 944-3611

In Canada
Embassy of the Kingdom of Thailand
180 Island Park Drive,
Ottawa, Ontario
Canada
K1Y 0A2
Ph. (613) 722-4444; Fax (613) 722-6624

Social Studies

3. Asian Medicine

For thousands of years, the people in Asia have been practicing healing in a markedly different way than traditional Western practitioners of medicine. The healing process involves the use of herbs, dietary restrictions, acupuncture, massage therapy, meditation, and, in some cases, shamanism.

Their pharmacopeia is highly developed with an array of over 1,800 items. Due to deep-rooted aversion in Asian cultures to the shedding of blood, combined with a belief that mutilation continues in the afterlife, surgery has never been extensively developed. Rather, external massage and micro-intrusive methods of heat and acupuncture therapies are used. Thai people have, over the centuries, engraved their knowledge in diverse subjects such as medicine, astronomy, history, social customs, and literature on their wats across the land.

Invite an Asian doctor or Western practitioner of alternative medicine to come and speak to your class about massage, acupuncture, and herbal therapies. Suggest to your guest speaker that a comparison of Asian medicine with western medicine would be of interest to your students.

4. Geography of Southeast Asia

The Kingdom of Thailand shares borders with Malaysia, Myanmar (Burma), Laos, and Cambodia. The country's east coast borders the Gulf of Thailand, and its west coast ends at the Andaman Sea.

Provide students with tracing paper. Ask them to trace the countries that make up Southeast Asia. Ask them to label the countries and their capital cities, and to color each country with a different color. This exercise will be critical for them to sort out the countries that occupy this parcel of land.

5. Cultural and Social Customs

Today, a Western visitor must be well prepared beforehand to avoid receiving culture shock once in Thailand. Monarchy and religion are revered in Thailand. An insult to either the Thai monarch or Thai beliefs is not tolerated. When the Thai national anthem is played, everybody is expected to stand alert (as in the West). The Thai king and the royal family are beyond reproach. The mildest form of criticism is treasonous. When visiting a temple, one must dress appropriately in modest clothing.

Brainstorm with your class about what is revered in our culture. List their suggestions on the chalkboard. What is the etiquette in which visitors to our country must be well versed (e.g., chewing quietly)? How tolerant are we if a visitor unknowingly violates one of our cultural or social norms?

6. Thai Ramakien and Indian Divali: A Cross-Cultural Celebration

In India, Divali celebrates Prince Rama's homecoming after his long odyssey and his conquest over evil, which took the form of a buffalo-headed creature. The Thai people celebrate the same cultural event, which shares its common roots in Indian Buddhism. They celebrate the Ramakien with a classical Thai dance. On the chapel doors of Wat Po in Bangkok, mother-of-pearl is inlaid to visually depict the Thai epic Ramakien, which tells of Prince Rama's safe return to his homeland.

Lead your class in brainstorming about the cultural, religious, or social celebrations we share with other cultures and/or countries.

7. World History: Universal Centers of Learning

"Walls that look like a giant textbook can be found at Wat Po in Bangkok, Thailand. Thai people call the temple Thailand's first open university because students used to come here to study."

Wat Po is a long established center of public education and is referred to as Thailand's First Open University. The temple is also the center of traditional medicine in Thailand. Stone plaques and inscriptions describe treatments for various ailments and show methods of massage and meditation.

A wat, a temple-monastery, serves as the guardian of religion, culture, and knowledge in Thailand. There are hundreds of wats in Thailand; each one is ornately decorated and respectfully cared for throughout history. In Europe, monasteries, rectories, cathedrals, and churches were also places of learning for aspirants to the monastic life and priesthood.

Lead your students in exploring the universal role played by monks and priests in providing education in Medieval Europe. Help them to compare and contrast how education was delivered in European monasteries and Thai wats.

Science

8. A Virtual Visitor's Weather Report

What is the weather today in Bangkok? What is the forecast for the next four days? Younger students may follow the daily weather in Bangkok and graph the results. Compare the temperatures to what you are experiencing in your part of the world. How is it different? Why? The address of the Intellicast site is:

URL: *http://www.intellicast.com/weather/bkk/*

Find "section 4—Intellicast sky—condition codes" (at the above Internet site) and print out, or copy, the symbols for the various weather conditions. White-out the descriptions and see how close the students can come to guessing their meaning. Conversely, give the students the weather conditions (cloudy, dust, foggy, hot, snow shower, thunderstorm, clear evening, very cold, etc.) and have them come up with symbolic codes. Show them the codes Intellicast uses, and compare.

Older students can access current satellite images of Asia (and around the world). Based on what they observe over a period of daily watching, can they predict when the next storm will hit Thailand? How accurate were they? (Check the weather for that day.)

Information is available at this site, for those who are interested, about satellite imagery, how it is used, and what the terms used mean, etc.

9. Tropical Storms: How Are They Formed?

Tropical storms are common in Thailand. Examine with your students how they develop, where they are more likely to be found, what the difference is (if any) between tropical storms over the Atlantic Ocean and over the Pacific Ocean, how people can know ahead of time when a storm is coming, and what people can do to protect themselves. Ample books and articles are listed in the bibliography to help your students with this study.

Mathematics

10. Estimation: The Mount Rushmore Heritage

The Mount Rushmore statues are known as the "shrine of democracy" where Americans celebrate the national spirit embodied in four presidents: Washington, the Father of the Nation; Lincoln, the Preserver of the Union; Jefferson, the Expansionist; and Roosevelt, Protector of the Working Man.

Show pictures or slides of the statues of U.S. presidents on Mount Rushmore. Ask your students to estimate the height of each sculpted head. Record their answers on a wall graph.

Ask them to write to Mount Rushmore National Memorial (see Activity #1) for brochures and facts sheets on "A Monument for the Ages." When the information arrives, ask students to check out their earlier estimations. Use a different color to place the actual height of each granite head on the graph.

Arts and Crafts

11. Three-Dimensional Art

As a follow-up to the above learning activity, provide students with an opportunity to sculpt with clay. With assistance of your art teacher, help your students to first each sketch on paper the face of a favorite person (this could be their parents, grandparents, folk heroes, favorite musician, sports icons).

Provide your students with carving tools and modelling clay (obtainable from arts-and-crafts stores, or play dough for younger students). You may also use home-made sawdust dough as a sculpting medium. (Please find a recipe for home-made modelling dough in the "Teacher's Notes" section of the chapter on the Dog Wall in Tokyo.)

With used newspaper spread out on their desks, students can mold and carve miniature busts of their favorite people. When done, let the statues dry for two days. Provide a time for students to show and tell about why their chosen persons are special to them.

Food Experience

12. Recipes

Coconut is common in Thailand, and a favorite ingredient for many dishes.

Thai Coconut Pancakes

Ingredients:

1 cup rice flour	3/4 cup shredded coconut
1/4 cup sugar	Vegetable oil
1/2 tsp. salt	Red and green food colors
1 can (14 oz.) unsweetened coconut milk	Sweetened condensed milk
4 eggs	More shredded coconut

Method

1. Beat flour, sugar, salt, coconut milk, and eggs in medium bowl until smooth.
2. Stir in 3/4 cup coconut.
3. Divide batter equally among three bowls.
4. Tint one part of batter pale pink with red food color, and one part pale green with green food color; leave the third part untinted.
5. Lightly oil an 8-inch non-stick skillet; heat until hot.
6. For each pancake, pour 1/4 cup batter into skillet and rotate skillets so batter covers bottom.
7. Cook until top is almost dry and bottom is light brown.
8. Run a wide spatula around edge to loosen; turn and cook other side until light brown.
9. Roll up pancake, place on heat proof platter, arrange the three colors one beside the other; keep warm.
10. Drizzle with sweetened condensed milk, and sprinkle with coconut.

Note: To use in the classroom, divide the class into groups of six or eight each. Each group can make one batch of pancakes, with the students in the groups taking turns at the stove, cooking them.

Used with permission from Sary Borquez of Edmonton, Alberta.

Internet Resources
13. Tour Thailand

Patrick Jennings has travelled extensively in Southeast Asia, Japan, and Australia, and always takes his laptop computer with him, complete with modem. We benefit from this because of his generous journalling and photo taking. If your students are too young to appreciate Mr. Jennings journals directly, you, as teacher, can certainly learn a lot about Thailand through them, which you can pass on to your class. To check it out, go to
URL: *http://www.whistler.net/worldtour/homepage/ejournal/ejtoc.htm*

Included are:
- Pay Dirt (an article about his experiences travelling with a computer in Thailand);
- The King and I (journal entries);
- Days of Brine and Islands (more journalling with photos);
- I wouldn't do that if I were you (etiquette in Thailand);
- Buddha's Top 10 Requirements for Those Who Govern;
- The Accidental Farang;
- Whoops! (about monks and stupa);
- Buddha Parties! (Patrick misses the event but describes the preparation for a major celebration);
- Image Gallery (search here for photos of Thailand, Bangkok, and Wat Po).

14. The Treasure That is Wat Po (Wat Phra Chetuphon)

Inside Wat Po (Temple of the Reclining Buddha), lies a reclining gold-plated Buddha, 150 feet (46 meters) long and 50 feet (15 meters) high. The mother-of-pearl inlay on the feet of the Buddha represents the 108 marks whereby Buddha is recognized. More mother-of-pearl is used on the chapel doors to depict scenes from the Thai epic Ramakien. The spire, called the Stupa, is encrusted with colorful porcelain.

You and your class can view the beauty of Wat Po in brilliant color by accessing this web site:
URL: *http://www.whistler.net/worldtour/homepage/gallery/watpho.htm*

Obtain from the library or friends slides of ornate temples, synagogues, mosques, and cathedrals (such as St., Peter's Basilica) around the world. Show students the slides and discuss why some places of worship in most faiths are so ornately decorated and treasure-laden.

Bibliography

See the bibliography for Tibet in the previous chapter for books on Buddhism.

Childcraft: The How and Why Library, Volume 4: World and Space, Field Enterprises Educational Corporation (Chicago), 1975. Information useful to younger children about weather (for the science activity).

Cooper, Robert and Nanthapa Cooper, *Culture Shock! Thailand*, Graphic Arts Center Publishing Company (Portland, Oregon), 1982. Chapter 9, "The Culture Game," could be quite fun for your students. Give your students the quiz on how to act in different social situations in Thailand. Then, using the commentary provided, explain how a polite person in Thailand would have behaved. (Now, be fair and test yourself, too!)

Frisky, Margaret, "The True Book of Air Around Us," *I Want to Know About....* Childrens Press (Chicago), 1972. The young reader can learn more about weather: facts about air, wind, weather maps, clouds, and weather activity such as rain, fog, hail, lightning, thunder, etc.

Goodman, Jim, *Cultures of the World: Thailand*, Marshall Cavendish (New York), 1993. Did you know that every Thai male is expected to spend a few months in a wat? Photos on every page show Thailand in contrast: old and modern, rural and urban, work and play. Grade 3+.

Grove, Noel, "The Many Faces of Thailand" *National Geographic*, February 1996. Thailand has taken on a faster pace in the last decade, bringing with it the problems of a huge sex industry, half the opium of the world funnelling through the country, deforestation, pollution, and overcrowding. This article looks at how the Thais are coping.

Growing up with Science: The Illustrated Encyclopedia of Invention, H.S. Stuttman (Westport, Connecticut), 1984. This 27-volume encyclopedia for children contains many articles useful for the science activities on weather: Barometers, vol. 2; Clouds, Communications Satellites, vol. 4; Meteorology, vol. 9; Tropical Cyclones, vol. 19; Weather forecasting, Weather systems, vol. 21; Air Pressure, Air Thermometer, Weather Indicator, Clouds, vol. 25.

Jacobsen, Karen, *Thailand*. Children's Book Press (Emeryville, CA), 1989.

Oliviero, Jamie, *Som See and the Magic Elephant*, Hyperion (New York), 1995. An original folktale set in Thailand.

O'Neil, Thomas, "The Mekong: A Haunted River's Season of Peace," *National Geographic*, February 1993. The Mekong River finds its headwaters in Tibet and forms the eastern border of Thailand before emptying through the Vietnam delta into the South China Sea.

Podendorf, Illa, "The True Book of Weather Experiments," *I Want to Know About....* Wonderfully easy activities based on weather for the primary student. The text also explains why the experiments work the way they do.

Thompson, Ruth and Neil, *A Family in Thailand*, Lerner Publications (New York), 1988. Part of the "Families the World Over" series.

Vesilind, Pruiit J., "Life-Breath of Half the World: Monsoons," *National Geographic*, December 1984. A wonderful resource for the science activity on tropical storms. Though Thailand doesn't get special mention in this article, it is smack-dab in the heart of the monsoon belt.

"Weather," *The Young Children's Encyclopedia, Volume 16*, Encyclopaedia Britannica, Inc. (Chicago), 1977. Carol is afraid of the thunder storm but her dad helps her to understand. Big winds such as hurricanes and tornados are explained, as well as clouds.

Wall 5 Hadrian's Wall: A Roman Signature in the United Kingdom

Pre-Reading Warm-Up

1. Critical Thinking

Reminiscent in both appearance and function to the Great Wall of China, Emperor Hadrian's defense system flanked one of the furthest boundaries of the Roman Empire.

Referring to a chapter on the Great Wall of China in *Talking Walls* and *Talking Walls Teacher's Guide* (published by Tilbury House, Publishers in 1992), present a lesson on the Great Wall of China. After the presentation, discuss with the class the similarities and differences of both historic defense systems, the Great Wall of China and Hadrian's Wall. Note the students' input on a sheet of chart paper.

Lead the class in identifying and discussing modern-day defense systems implemented by many nations, such as radar early warning systems (e.g., DEW Line), satellite detection systems, etc.

Identify defense systems in your community. How are they implemented and what are they for? Discuss.

Language Arts

2. Debate

Hadrian's Wall was built as a barrier in Northern England about 2,000 years ago. Some historians say it was built to keep people out, but others are still wondering if it kept people in.

Provide your class with reference sources and a bibliography on the subject of Hadrian's Wall. (Please refer to the bibliography at the conclusion of this chapter.)

Arrange your students in groups of three. Instruct them to conduct research on Hadrian's Wall for the purpose of debating on the motion: "That Emperor Hadrian built the wall to keep the rebel Britons out of his Roman colony." Groups will select opposing views for the debate. You may wish to invite parents and school officials to watch the students debate.

3. Fiction Writing

Engage your students in re-creating the life of a Roman soldier guarding the northernmost frontier of the Empire. Ask them to consider the following questions:

A) Might guarding the wall have been busy, rewarding, or lonely?

B) Would the job have been a perk or a drudge?

C) Would the soldiers have wished they were home in Rome?

Ask them to pretend that they are Roman soldiers performing their historic peace-keeping duties in a foreign land away from home and family. Have them write journals and letters to their parents, wives, children, or sweethearts at home.

4. Letter Writing

Encourage your students to write to the following for information and brochures on the archaeological findings of Hadrian's Wall.

Percival Turnbull,
Orchard Cottage,
Dalton, North Richmond,
Yorkshire, DL11 7HY
England Watertown, MA 02272
Ph. (0833) 621334

Dr. Andrew Hudson, Acting Executive Director
Jim Chairelli, Program Director
The Center for Field Research, Earthwatch
680 Mt. Auburn Street, Box 403
USA
Ph. (800) 776-0188; Fax (617) 926-8532\
E-mail: *cfr@earthwatch.org*

Social Studies

5. Re-Enactments of Historic Events

"Once a year, English children dress up as Roman soldiers and pretend to march and guard Hadrian's Wall."

What purpose do ceremonial re-enactments, in period costumes, of historical events serve?

Is history re-enacted in your area? Lead your class in identifying and discussing ceremonial re-enactments of historical events or places in your community and country. Would they like to create their own historical re-enactment?

6. World Geography

From historical and archaeological evidence, we know that Roman Emperor Hadrian built the 74-mile (119- km) fortified wall from Wallsend on England's east coast to Bowness-on-Solway at the coast of Solway Firth on the west, with an extension of fortresses down to the Cumbria coast for several miles, perhaps to defend the mainland against invasion by the rebel Britons from Galloway and Ireland.

Ask the students to locate on a map of the United Kingdom where the east and west terminals of Hadrian's Wall were. Provide each group of students with a topographical map of England, a blank sheet of overhead projection transparency acetate, and a water-soluble overhead projection pen. Instruct each group to re-trace, with reference to the topographies, the location of Hadrian's Wall on the acetate sheet.

7. "Walls That Divide": A Study of Boundaries

After the debate (Language Arts Activity #2), help students apply their learning to real-life situations by leading a discussion and guided exploration on places in the world where fortified walls and/or invisible boundaries (as between the U.S. and Canada or the U.S. and Mexico) are used to keep people separated from each other. Also, consider those places around the world where walls and boundaries have been dismantled (as between East and West Germany) for a freer flow of populations.

8. World History

Prepare a series of lessons on the Rise and Fall of the Roman Empire. Trace the expansion of the Empire to other parts of Europe.

Lead your class in examining the political, geographic, military, social, and economic meanings of colonization. Identify the political colonies of nations around the world today. Is the New World a result of colonization by European nations? Discuss.

Has your country ever been colonized? By whom? If not, why not?

Has your country ever colonized another land? Which one(s)?

9. Research Project

The excavated remains of Hadrian's Wall are recognized by the United Nations as a World Heritage Site, selected for preservation. Conduct research as to how many places/antiquities around the world are identified and recognized as World Heritage Sites. Are there any in your country or region? What and where are they? Why were they chosen? Should there be others?

Science

10. Wetlands

"During the last 20 years English Heritage and its predecessor, the Department of the Environment, have been involved in archaeological projects initiated to investigate the wetlands of England in a systematic way." (John Dodds of Lancaster University Archaeological Unit) Extensive archaeological deposits are endangered by agencies wishing to exploit the peat bogs. Because of their high acidity, these bogs are able to preserve even the very faces of our ancestors as well as artifacts.

Look at the bogs and wetlands of England as well as those at home. Why are wetlands important? How do they contribute to our environment? Why would they preserve so well? What plant life makes up the bogs and wetlands? If you live close enough, visit a wetland near you. Examine the plant life; take dipnets and identification guides to look at the aquatic insect life of the bog. Eat some cranberries and enjoy one of the bounties of the North American bog. (See the bibliography at the end of this chapter for some resources.)

Mathematics

11. Roman Numerals

At the time Hadrian's Wall was built, people were using what we now refer to as Roman Numerals. Take this opportunity to teach this different notational system. Young children may only learn the numbers to 20, whereas older students may be given complicated numbers to decipher. Tailor this activity to the abilities of your class. Below are the key numerals to know:

I = 1	XI = 11	CX = 110
II = 2	XIV = 14	CC = 200
III = 3	XV = 15	CD = 400
IV = 4	XIX = 19	D = 500
V = 5	XX = 20	DC = 600
VI = 6	XL = 40	CM = 900
VII = 7	L = 50	M = 1,000
VIII = 8	LX = 60	MXL = 1,040
IX = 9	XC = 90	
X = 10	C = 100	

12. Measurement—Linear (A)

As a lesson in community study and geometry, provide every group of three students with a neighborhood map and a geometry compass. Using the distance scale on the map and the compass, instruct students to measure and mark a one-mile (1.6-km) circumference on the map, with the school as the center. Ask groups to identify major community landmarks (a public library, a hospital, a community club, a police station, a church, another school, a historical site, etc.) at the one-mile circumference. On the chalk board or on chart paper, write the names of the identified places on one column. On the second column poll the place to which the majority of the class would like to visit.

Arrange a brisk one-mile (1.6-km) walk for your class on a separate day, using your school as the starting point. If applicable, prior to the field trip contact the management of your destination site for permission and arrangements for the intended visit. Upon arrival at the one-mile location, remind the students that Hadrian's Wall was over 70 times the distance they have just completed. The exercise would provide your students with a concept of the size of Hadrian's Wall.

13. Measurement—Linear (B)

Hadrian's Wall stretched out 74 miles (119 km) in Northern England as a frontier defence system to separate the Romans from the Britons who refused to be under Roman rule.

Through an exercise in map reading, help students to obtain a clearer and more concrete concept of the length of Hadrian's Wall by asking them to identify on a map of their state/province/territory/country, two large population centers that are approximately 74 miles apart by the most direct route.

Alternatively, locate those places that are 74 miles from your school.

Arts and Crafts

14. Build the Wall

Ask students to collect 100 empty half-gallon (or one-liter) milk cartons. Assuming that each milk carton is approximately one mile in length, build a scale model of Hadrian's Wall with a fort turret every one mile (fashion the forts out of milk cartons as well) on the gym floor. Tape the milk cartons together with masking tape. Give the scale model a coat of tempera water-based paint that gives the appearance of an ancient fortified wall. The activity gives your students a proportional perspective of the size of the historic structure.

Food Experience

15. Recipe

Imagine a Roman soldier at Hadrian's Wall nipping down to the nearest McDonald's at the end of his watch. No, there was no Arch Deluxe, but the local inn probably made a mean Isicia Omentata, the next best thing.

Isicia Omentata (a kind of Roman burger)

Ingredients:
> 1 pound ground meat
> 1 French roll, made into crumbs, soaked in white grape juice
> 1/2 teaspoon freshly ground pepper
> 1/2 teaspoon salt
> 3 tablespoons white grape juice
> some pine nuts
> a little Caroenum (boil 1 cup of white grape juice until it is only 1/2 cup)

Method:
1. Combine meat and soaked bread.
2. Add salt, pepper, grape juice, mixing in well.
3. Form into small burgers.
4. Put pine nuts into each.
5. Grill the burgers, basting them with the Caroenum. (If no grill is available, use the broiler in the oven or fry them in a pan.)
6. Serve (with French rolls if desired, but no ketchup, mustard, or relish).

Internet Resources

16. Hadrian's Wall Country

Northumberland, England, bills itself as the place "where past and future meet." Though this Internet site is aimed primarily at tourist promotion, there is also some good information and photographs of the wall, artifacts found in the area, and regional scenery. To access, go to
URL: *http://www.demon.co.uk:80/tynedale/*

17. Museum of Antiquities

The Museum of Antiquities in England houses valuable artifacts from the Roman era of Great Britain. Their Internet site displays a generous sample of these items with full color photographs and is well worth visiting. Go to
URL: *http://www.ncl.ac.uk/~nantiq/index.html*

Find here:

• Reconstruction of a temple to Mithras (based on the first temple at Carrawburgh on Hadrian's Wall);
• Virtual Library for Object-of-the-Month (and previous months' entries) with commentary on its historical significance and use, e.g.,
   • Three altars to Antenociticus
   • The Capheaton Hanging Bowl
   • Cameo of a Bear
   • Sestertius of Hadrian
   • The Bronze Dodecahedron
   • The Aemilia Ring
   • Others
• Across the curriculum (aimed for ages 7 to 11). Though this is "a teacher's guide to further work in the classroom following a visit to the Museum of Antiquities," the activities are certainly relevant and adaptable for those too far away to actually set foot in the museum. Here you will find activities based on:
   • Technology—Make a model of the Roman water system;
   • Art—A mural of Roman life, fashion, and the British resistance;
   • Religious Education—The Mithraeum;
   • History—How British society was shaped by invading peoples;
   • Problem-Solving—The Roman Crossing.

18. Earthwatch at Milefortlet 21

"They hope that some of the Roman artifacts that they have found—jewelry, toys, sandals, and games—will be the clues they need to piece together more stories about Hadrian's Wall."

An environmental conservation group known as Earthwatch (680 Mt. Auburn St., P.O. Box 403, Watertown, MA, 02272; Ph. 800-775-0188; Fax 617- 926-8532) conducted an archaeological excavation at Milefortlet 21, one of the forts along the Wall just north of Mayport, Cumbria, in order to determine the exact layout, function, and occupation period of the stronghold, as well as the lifestyle of the fort's troops.

Guide your students to access the latest findings arising from these excavations by communicating with the Center for Field Research of Earthwatch through their electronic mail address: *cfr@earthwatch.org*. (At the time of writing, the Internet site was inaccessible).

19. Roman Fort on Tyne

Beginning in 1995, Earthwatch began another archeological dig relating to Hadrian's Wall. The Roman Fort on the mouth of the River Tyne protected the easternmost portion of the defense system. Earthwatch hopes to answer these questions:

• What was the role of the fort for the Roman army?
• Was it part of a typical system of military occupation, or was it part of a defense of the provinces against outside attack?
• Did the Romans affect the local agricultural practices or economy?

To learn more about this project, including some pictures, please see   the following Internet sites:

URL: *http://www.earthwatch.org/x/Xbidwell.html*

URL: *http://www.earthwatch.org/ed/bidwell/rf.html*

(One page only, this site is a simple description by a teacher of her experience working at the dig.)

URL: *http://www.earthwatch.org/g/Gbidwell.html*

(The objectives, fieldwork method, and results are recorded here.)

Teacher's Notes

Milecastles of Hadrian's Wall

At intervals of one Roman mile (about 1.6 km), "milecastles" were built to provide accommodations for Roman soldiers and a passageway for monitored entries and exits to the Roman colony. Traders used the milecastles as points of entry, so marketplaces developed in assigned locations near "Milecastles." Smaller "milefortlets" which served the same purpose as "milecastles" guarded the Cumbria coast without the protection of a wall. Milefortlet 21 is now the only element of Hadrian's coastal defenses of the northwest frontier of the Roman Empire to have been wholly excavated.

Bibliography

Adler, David A., *Roman Numerals*, Thomas Y. Crowell (New York), 1977. A useful picture books for teaching your youngest students about Roman numerals. It also contains an activity that makes learning this notation system easier. Grade 1+.

Allen, Kenneth, *One Day in Roman Britain*, Tyndall (England), 1973. This easy-flowing narrative follows five people through their day with accurate detail on the period. Well illustrated. Grade 3+.

"Archaeological Techniques," *Growing up with Science: The Illustrated Encyclopedia of Invention, Volume 1*, H.S. Stuttman (Westport, Connecticut), 1984. Of particular interest here is an aerial photograph which clearly indicates the site of a Roman Fort not yet excavated, but visible from the air by the different contours in the land. Underwater archaeology is also discussed.

"England," *The Young Children's Encyclopedia, Volume 5: Caves to Skyscrapers*, Encyclopaedia Britannica, Inc. (Chicago), 1977. When friends from another country come to visit, Johnny Atkins, whose parents own the Crown and Thistle Inn in Burford, gets to tour the United Kingdom with them (and the reader gets to join as well). Other information about England given as well.

Fox, Aileen, *Roman Britain*, Lutterworth Press (London), 1968. Wonderful black and white drawings illustrate this book. It looks at many aspects of Roman life in Britain. Grade 4+.

"The Head of the World," *The Young Children's Encyclopedia, Volume 5: Caves to Skyscrapers*, Encyclopaedia Britannica, Inc. (Chicago), 1977. A small village of mud huts grew up to rule the world. Hadrian's luxurious villa near Tivoli, Italy, is one of several places described.

Jorde-Johnston, James, *Hadrian's Wall*, Michael Joseph (London), 1977. This book for adults presents a complete history of the wall, including what life was like along the wall in the time of the Romans. Informative illustrations.

Levanthes, Louise, "Mysteries of the Bog," *National Geographic*, March 1987. What kind of wetlands are there? What is the plant life? Why are bogs considered cursed? Levanthes answers these questions and looks at the bodies found in bogs including details of one bog in central Florida. Bogs also provide life through the use of peat for heat and medical assistance.

Mairson, Alan, "The Everglades: Dying for Help," *National Geographic*, April 1994. The Everglades is one wetland that is gasping for life. This article provides an excellent resource for those students studying wetlands as a science activity.

Mitchell, John, "Our Disappearing Wetlands," *National Geographic*, October 1992. "Long dismissed as noxious, unprofitable places, wetlands are now prized as one of the richest ecosystems on earth. And yet their destruction continues." Included is a fold-out map of the United States, showing the wetlands of America from the Pacific to the Atlantic, from North Dakota to the Everglades. The photographs show the diversity of wetlands and their plant and animal life.

"Romans: Rulers of the Western World," *The Young Children's Encyclopedia, Volume 13*, Encyclopaedia Britannica, Inc. (Chicago), 1977. How did the Roman Empire begin and how did it grow to such power?

Salway, Peter, *The Oxford Illustrated History of Roman Britain*, Oxford University Press (New York), 1993. "This lavishly illustrated book presents the most authorative history of Roman Britain every published for the general reader." A chapter on Hadrianic Britain is especially pertinent to your classroom study.

Sorrell, Alan, *Roman London*, B.T. Batsford (London), 1969. Eighteen historical reconstruction drawings are accompanied by photographs artifacts to give a vivid picture of life in London throughout the Roman occupation. Grades 6+ will gain from reading the text, but even grade 1 will learn from the illustrations.

Sutcliff, Rosemary, *The Capricorn Bracelet*, Oxford University Press (London), 1973. The bracelet is an heirloom passed through a family of soldiers who each, in their turn, serve on or north of Hadrian's Wall. This is a collection of six stories. Grade 5+.

Sutcliff, Rosemary, *The Eagle of the Ninth*. Puffin Books, (Harmondsworth, England), 1977. "When a man's father has disappeared together with an entire legion and is accused of cowardice, it is natural that his son should want to reclaim his honor. So Marcus embarks on the perilous journey north of Hadrian's Wall, hoping not only to solve a mystery but to rediscover the famous Eagle, symbol of the Legion's honour." Grade 5+.

Sutcliff, Rosemary, *Frontier Wolf*, Oxford University Press (New York), 1980. A centurion is sent to take command of a force of scouts who have a bad reputation. The job is to maintain peace among the warrior tribes north of Hadrian's Wall. Grade 5+.

Sutcliff, Rosemary, *The Lantern Bearers*. Puffin Books, (Harmondsworth, England) 1981 "The Saxon raiding party did a thorough job when they attacked the farm—by morning it was a smoking ruin and Aquila's father lay dead alongside the household of servants. Bitter years followed for Aquila as he sought to revenge his father—and to keep alight the lantern of Roman civilization in the dark days of the barbarian invasions.... One of Rosemary Sutcliff's finest novels of Roman Britain, *The Lantern Bearers* was awarded the Carnegie Medal." Grade 5+.

Sutcliff, Rosemary, *The Silver Branch*, Oxford University Press (London), 1966. Sutcliff has an amazing gift in capturing the past and making it live again. This novel takes us to Hadrian's Wall and back to the south a hundred years before the Roman's left Britain. This is the second book in a loose trilogy comprised of *The Eagle of the Ninth* and *The Langern Bearers*. Grade 5+.

"Wetland Wilderness," *Disney's Wonderful World of Knowledge Yearbook 1988*, Grolier Enterprises (Danbury, Connecticut), 1988. Marshes, bogs, and swamp are all examined along with the threats to them outlined. Great photographic illustration of the difference between the three kinds of wetlands.

"The World Builders of Ancient Rome," *Disney's Wonderful World of Knowledge Volume 19: Art Through the Ages*, Danbury Press (Danbury, Connecticut), 1973. Many of Rome's structures were real works of art and there are plenty of them to look at in this article, along with an easy history of the Romans.

Wall 6 The Holocaust: A Dark Chapter In the History of Man

Pre-Reading Warm-Up

1. Exploring Social and Cultural Customs

"It is a Jewish custom for families and friends to leave a stone when they visit a grave." The custom signifies the respect-payer's remembrance of the departed. The placing of a rock by the graveside communicates the sentiment : "I've been here, and I'm not forgetting you." Historically, rocks placed at the gravesite served two objectives: to mark the gravesite and to protect the grave from desecrators.

Social customs and cultural traditions are symbols of our beliefs. Examples are standing erect at the playing of the national anthem, bowing the head at a moment of silent prayer or remembrance, giving of gifts at major celebrations such as wedding, birthday, graduation, baptism, and bar mitzvah, just to name a few.

Explore with your students the social customs and cultural traditions they and their families practice. First of all, brainstorm with your class about the social, religious, and cultural events and/or occasions that they celebrate. Write the list of occasions/events on the chalkboard. Have the students make a worksheet with five columns on it. Ask students to select five occasions/events at which customs are practiced.

Using the five occasions/events as column headings, instruct your students to write down as many customs associated with the occasions/events as they can. An example: under the heading of *birthday*, one can write: good wishes, gifts, party, special dinner, cards, family celebration, photographs, etc.

When your class is finished with the individual exercise, make a master chart of customs and traditions by collecting and collating your students' ideas on chart paper in their respective columns. This activity will open the door to inter-cultural understanding and acceptance of diversity among our students.

2. An Exercise in Discussing Stereotyping and Prejudice

Write the sentence fragments listed below on the chalkboard. Ask your students to complete the sentences. Help them reflect on possibly having formed stereotypes and prejudices in their responses to the following.

A) All teachers are

B) Sam is often late for school because

C) All male nurses are

D) Nobel Laureates are

E) Airline pilots are

F) All rap singers are

G) Single parents are

H) All televangelists are

I) The CEO of Xerox must be

J) All retirees are

Language Arts

3. Poetry:

After your students have studied the Holocaust, ask them to write either a poem or a mini-memoir describing how they would have felt had they been survivors of the Holocaust.

4. Responsive Writing:

Provide your students with photographs of Europe and of concentration camps before, during, and after the war (Susan D. Bachrach's *Tell Them We Remember: The Story of the Holocaust* contains many photographs for this purpose). Ask them to write responses and impressions either in prose or poetry. See the bibliography at the end of this chapter for more information on Susan Bachrach's book.

5. Responsive Listening:

A) Read to your class the famous children's story, *The Emperor's New Clothes*, and discuss with your students the lesson of the story. Ask them to apply it to the true occurrences where on-lookers simply keep their eyes closed and their mouths shut.

B) Provide your class with the song lyrics of Simon and Garfunkel's famous song, "Sounds of Silence." Play the song and discuss what the song says.

6. Oral Discussion:

Explore the following ideas with your students:

What is the literal meaning of "holocaust" (fire that destroys)?

What is meant by the Holocaust as a historic event?

What is meant by the term "hate crimes"? Why do they happen? How do we stop hate crimes?

What are some reasons for hatred among people and groups?

What was the "Nazi Ideal"? Why was this idea so destructive?

Are these so-called "ideals" still perpetuated by groups today? By whom? How?

For older students, ask if the KKK and Neo-Nazis have anything in common?

What can we do about the so-called "Neo-Nazi activities" in Europe and North America? Are we going to be the deathly silent bystanders again this time around? What can we do about the current problems?

What are the most glaring instances of genocide or human rights abuses happening now in the world? (Former Yugoslavia, China, Rwanda, Somalia, etc.)

How does racism play a role in human destructiveness? What about sexism? Anti-semitism? Agism? Classism? Are there any other "-isms" you can think of ?

Some people say that this society is fascinated by and obsessed with sex, horror, gore, destruction, perversion, death, and murder in the media and entertainment. Is this fascination positive or negative in the total scheme of human affairs? Why? What can we do about it?

Social Studies

7. Yom Ha-Shoah (Holocaust Memorial Day)

Yom Ha-Shoah (Holocaust Memorial Day) is a day in the Jewish calendar designated as a day to commemorate the Holocaust. It occurs in spring and is determined by the Jewish calendar. Invite a member of your local Jewish community to come and talk to your class about the Holocaust and how the Jewish people commemorate this day.

8. Children and the Holocaust: An Empathy-Development Exercise

About 1.5 million children were murdered during the Holocaust in occupied Europe. Of this figure, over 1.2 million were Jewish children, tens of thousands were Gypsy children, and thousands of institutionalized handicapped children were also murdered. Children were persecuted along with their families for racial, religious, or political reasons.

In 1935, laws proclaimed at Nuremberg stripped German Jews of their citizenship. They suddenly found themselves become non-persons, with no economic, political, legal, or social standing. Among children, close friends suddenly avoided the company of their Jewish classmates, sometimes becoming unfriendly and hostile. In 1938, German Jewish children were prohibited from attending German schools. This same measure also applied for Gypsy children as well.

Lead your class in discussing what their feelings would have been if they were the Jewish children who were suddenly treated as "nobodies" by their friends. Take them back in time to the segregated schools system in the U.S. not too many years ago. Talk further about those inequities. Are there any inequities that children are subjected to today? Discuss.

Activity #5 in the "Dikes in the Netherlands" section focuses on the story of Anne Frank; it includes an Internet site and the address of the Anne Frank House in Amsterdam. You may wish to use this activity here.

9. The Struggles of Minorities

Assign students to compare and contrast the Holocaust to the struggle of other groups, such as the aboriginal peoples of the Americas, African Americans, and other ethnic minorities. Consider also the struggle of the Tibetans for independence from the Chinese colonists.

10. National Boundary Changes

Using pre- and post-World War II maps, discuss the changes in national boundaries in Europe.

11. Conspiracy of Silence

With the first thunderous salutation of "Heil Hitler!" in 1933 came the first whisper of fear in Jewish homes in Germany. From then on and for the next twelve years, unspeakable horror visited millions of human beings under a pall of wide-eyed silence spoken by an equally large number of "bystanders." Silence, indifference, and apathy to human suffering and the infringement of human rights in any society can only serve to perpetuate those problems, like a co-conspirator or accessory to the crime.

Discuss with your class the sociological phenomenon of the "conspiracy of silence." Explore with them the instances of "conspiracy of silence" in heinous crimes throughout history, in the recent past, and at the present moment. Some glaring examples are the silent witnesses of the Holocaust, the inaction of the Allies for the first few years of the Holocaust, the steady stream of noon-hour passersby who silently witnessed the murder of a man in downtown New York, the conspiracy of silence in the rape-murder of a Cree school girl in a small northern town in Manitoba, Canada, and the silence of the Western powers in human rights abuses exercised by the Chinese government on its dissidents and Tibetans.

12. Genocide Then and Now

Discuss with your class the parallelism between the Holocaust and modern-day genocide as found in the former Yugoslavia, Bosnia-Herzgovenia, China, Rwanda, Burundi, and Somalia.

13. Compare Government Styles

Assign an expository essay comparing an authoritarian government with a democratic system. Ask students to substantiate their comparisons with current examples.

14. See also "Internet Resources" towards the end of this chapter

Science

15. Science Ethics

Discuss the following topics of science with your older students:

A. The ethics of genetic engineering, such as test tube babies, biotechnology, and Hitler's Eugenics (selection of racial purity);

B. The pseudo-science of racial classification of superiority;

C. The inhumane practice of medical experiments carried out in concentration camps by Nazi scientists and doctors such as Joseph Mengele;

D. The scientific fallacies that Jews are a race, that handicapped people are inferior, and that the Aryan race is superior.

16. See also "Internet Resources" towards the end of this chapter.

Mathematics

17. Number Operations—Multiplication

Using the population size of your community (city or town), compute how many times your community would have to be multiplied to equal the number of innocent people who were murdered in the Holocaust (approximately 12 million).

18. Calculator Usage

Most people are unable to grasp numbers as large as one million. Ask students to calculate how long it would take them to count to one million if they counted one number for each second. Ask them to compute how long it would take to count to 12 million. That's the approximate number of innocent people who were murdered during the Holocaust. They would have the concept that one person was being murdered for each second they counted.

19. Data Management—Graphing

Using a graph, help your students with numerical comparisons between genocides of the Native Americans, Armenians, Cambodians, Rwandans, Tibetans, Bosnians and Serbians—and that of the Holocaust.

20. See also "Internet Resources" towards the end of this chapter.

Arts and Crafts

21. Build a Stone Wall

Have each student bring to class the name, birthdate, and death date of someone they know and/or are related to. (A great-grandparent is usually distant enough if anyone else causes too much pain to remember. Conversely, the students can invent names and dates but this would not be as meaningful.) Take the students on a walk or field trip to look for stones. Bring the stones back into the classroom and, with thick white and/or black paint and thin brushes, have the students each turn a stone into a memorial. Now, using cement as mortar (cement powder is available at building stores—just add water and stir!), build a small wall in the classroom.

Food Experience

22. Recipe

The Sabbath is a day holy to observant Jews around the world. From sunset Friday until sunset Saturday no work may be done. When fireplaces and wood-burning stoves were used to heat the home, many Polish Jews had willing Gentiles take care of their fires so that they would not freeze on the Sabbath. Cholent is a meal-in-one that can be prepared the day before and served on the Day of Rest.

Cholent

Ingredients:

2 onions, diced
2 tablespoons vegetable shortening or chicken fat
1/2 pound dried lima beans, soaked overnight in cold water
1/2 cup barley
6 to 8 raw potatoes, pared and quartered
2 pounds brisket of beef, in one piece
2 tablespoons all-purpose flour
Salt, pepper and paprika to taste
Boiling water

Method:

1. Brown onions in fat in large heavy pan.
2. Add presoaked beans, barley and potatoes.
3. Make a space in the center and place the meat there.
4. Mix flour and seasonings together.
5. Sprinkle seasoned flour over the meat and vegetables.
6. Add boiling water (it should fill the pan nearly to the top).
7. Cover tightly and simmer on very low heat (you could use an asbestos pad between the stove element and the pan).
8. Cook for 5 hours or overnight. Do not stir, but shake the pan from time to time to prevent sticking.
9. Serve.

Note: You may prefer to use an electric slow cooker or a 200°F oven overnight.

Internet Resources

23. The United States Holocaust Memorial Museum

If you are unable to take your class to the Memorial Museum (see #27 below), the next best way to visit it is through the Internet.

URL: *http://www.ushmm.org/index.html*

When you arrive at the museum's homepage, go to "Learning about the Holocaust." This "page" includes:

- Guidelines for Teaching about the Holocaust
  - Why teach Holocaust history?
  - Questions of rationale;
  - Methodological considerations;
  - Incorporating a study of the Holocaust into existing courses;
- A brief history of the Holocaust;
- Five questions (and answers) about the Holocaust;
  - What was the Holocaust?
  - Who were the Nazis?
  - Why did the Nazis want to kill large numbers of innocent people?
  - How did the Nazis carry out their policy of genocide?
  - How did the world respond to the Holocaust?
- Children and the Holocaust
- Much more (check out the site's Table of Contents for the complete list).

24. Cybrary of the Holocaust

URL: *http://www.remember.org/*

The Cybrary of the Holocaust is dedicated to educating people around the world about the horrors of the Holocaust. It is part of a two-year educational project which began with a trip to Israel and will conclude with CD-ROM for educational use at no cost.

At this excellent Internet site, maintained by Michael Declan Dunn (*mddunn@best.com*) of the Write Thing, you will find links to:

- "Put Hate on Hold" by Harold Gordon (with audio clips);
- "The Truth About Anne Frank—Twelve-Hour Class Outline (some great teaching ideas here);
- "A Day of Work at Dachau Camp 2" from the prize-winning book *How Dark the Heavens* by Sidney Iwens;
- "Keep Yelling" by Maurie Hoffman, whose mother insisted he run from annihilation (photos included);
- Information about seminars for educators, of primary to university students, who teach about the Holocaust;
- Auschwitz/Birkenau photos by Alan Jacobs;
- *Abe's Story* (see #25 below);
- Facts (The complete instruction guide created by Gary Brobman with a multitude of links. This is worth spending time in. It is excellent.);
- Witnesses' stories (including survivors, resistence workers, victims, perpetrators, and liberators);
- Holocaust and Genocide Curriculum for K-12 (separated into K-3, 4-6, 7-12).
- Many, many more topics and links than there is space to relate here.

25. Putting a Face on the Holocaust: Abe's Story

Abram Korn had survived the horrors of the Holocaust through sheer will. He immigrated to America and, through his usual determination, built a successful automobile business. He had almost completed a rough draft of his memoir of his unspeakable Holocaust years by the time he died in 1972. Joseph Korn, his eldest son, picked up where his father had left off. He recently prepared Abe's manuscript for publication. *Abe's Story: A Holocaust Memoir* was released on April 11, 1995, the fiftieth anniversary of Abe's liberation from Buchenwald Concentration Camp. *Abe's Story* places a human face on the incredible nightmare to which millions of people had been subjected over a period of ten years in human history. You may order your copy of *Abe's Story* by e-mailing Joseph Korn (*joeyk@csra.net* or *JWKorn@aol.com*).

An Internet site has been established, based on the book, with an interactive map, excerpts from *Abe's Story*, and teaching tools that can be quite useful to the classroom, whether you have the book or not.

URL: *http://www/remember.org/abe/*

"Teaching Tools" contains "activities to help the students learn more about the world they live in today and about the dangers of hate and prejudice in the world and in their lives. It will help the students realize that we all have the potential for good and evil in any circumstances; the choice is ours to make." In this unit of study, excellent learning activities are suggested for classroom use in

Language Arts,
Social Studies,
Mathematics,
Science/Health,
Art,
Music/Drama.

26. An Electronic Interdisciplinary Unit on the Holocaust: "The Beast Within"

A team of dedicated educators, from North Hagerstown High School in Maryland, has listed an interdisciplinary unit on the Holocaust, entitled "The Beast Within." Maintained by their grade 9 students, the unit assists students in studying "the darker side of human nature" as explored by the literature and history of 20th-century man.
URL: *http://www.fred.net/nhhs/html/beast.htm*

The topics of "The Beast Within: An Interdisciplinary Unit" consists of those in the four core disciplines: social studies, English language arts, science, and mathematics.

Social Studies:

• Examine the human rights abuses of such regimes as Nazi Germany, Iraq under Saddam Hussein, Cuba under Fidel Castro, and China under the Communist party;
• Link to the United States Holocaust Memorial Museum:
URL: *http://www.ushmm.org/*
• Check out grade 9 students' comments on their visit to the Museum;
• Link to news and issues surrounding Bosnia, including a map of the former Yugoslavia as it is now.

English:

• A list of literature that illustrates the darker side of man's free will;
• Link to Holocaust glossary: terms, places, and personalities:
URL: *http://www.wiesenthal.com/resource/gloss.htm*
• Link to Hilve Firek's "Teaching the Holocaust" page, which itself links to:
  • The United States Holocaust Memorial Museum (see above);
  • The Cybrary of the Holocaust (an excellent site: see #24 above);
  • The Simon Wiesenthal Center;
  • The Museum of Tolerance;
  • Yad Vashaem;
  • The Holocaust/Genocide Project;
  • Auschwitz—A Layman's Guide to Auschwitz-Birkenau;
  • Syllabi for teaching the Holocaust;
  • The Anne Frank House (includes pictures);
  • A list of discussion questions.

Science:

• Elements for discussion.

Mathematics:

• Develop line, bar, circle, or pictographs illustrating some statistical application of Holocaust data (suggestions of possible applications given);

Miscellaneous:

• Suggested assignments for students that would pull together all they've learned about the Holocaust;
• Students' poetry and prose on the subject;
• Students from other schools may, under certain conditions, have their comments, poetry, essays, and/or graphic art posted to this site.
• Links to other Holocaust sites.

A personal note:

Mr. George Cassuto, one of the teachers of "The Beast Within," told this author that, during the Holocaust, his mother was hidden and rescued by a "righteous gentile," a Christian who felt it was her duty to protect innocent children during the Holocaust. On a wall dedicated to Holocaust rescuers in the United States Holocaust Memorial Museum in Washington, DC, Mrs. Cassuto's rescuer, Grietje Bogaarts, has her name inscribed on the wall.

Mr. Cassuto named his oldest daughter, aged two, after her grandmother's rescuer, Grietje. Grietje means "grace" in English, Mr. Cassuto feels it was by the grace of God that his parents survived the Holocaust.

To get in touch with Mr. Cassuto about his family history and/or about "The Beast Within: An Interdisciplinary Unit," you may e-mail: *nhhs@fred.net*.

Community Resources

27. Plan a Visit to the United States Holocaust Memorial Museum

The United States Holocaust Memorial Museum is America's living memorial to the six million Jews and millions of other victims who perished during the Holocaust. The Museum also serves as a national institution for documentation, study, education, and interpretation of Holocaust history.

Among its permanent exhibits are original documents, oral histories, photographs, documentary film, and artifacts of the Holocaust. The exhibition also highlights stories of resistance and rescue. The Hall of Remembrance serves as the national memorial to the victims of the Holocaust. The Museum houses the Learning Center, an interactive computer-based environment that guides the visitor through the events and issues of the Holocaust. The Holocaust Research Institute includes a library, an archive, a theater, and an auditorium. A special exhibition gallery offers changing displays on subjects complementary to the permanent exhibit.

Two galleries are dedicated to children's education. "Daniel's Story" is an exhibition intended for children aged 8 to 13. A Children's Wall in the Museum's education center, featuring 3,000 tiles hand-painted by American school children, commemorates the approximately 1.5 million children who died in the Holocaust.

As a long-term project, with the approval of your school administration, school district, P.T.A., and community, organize a fund-raising campaign towards a trip to visit the USHMM in Washington.

In the meantime, encourage your students to communicate with the education department of the Museum with regards to the Holocaust, particularly with reference to the plight of children caught in the maelstrom of the tragedy.

You may contact the United States Holocaust Memorial Museum at its e-mail address: *web administrator@ushmm.org* or write to the Museum at the address below.

Teacher's Notes

The Holocaust is such a significant and tragic chapter in human history that innumerable pages have been written about it. As an institution of education and cultural transmission, the school has a responsibility to teach young people what happened in the Holocaust so that similar mistakes will not occur again in our or their generations.

Many fine curricula have been developed to teach the Holocaust in a sensitive, meaningful, and productive way. Please feel free to contact the following for further assistance in teaching the Holocaust.

The Education Department,
United States Holocaust Memorial Museum,
100 Raoul Wallenberg Place, SW

Washington, DC 20024,
USA
Ph. (202)488-0400

See the note about the museum's *Teaching About the Holocaust: A Resource Guide for Educators* in the bibliography below.

Bibliography

Note: You should be sure that the Holocaust materials you present to your class are appropriate to the age of the children you are teaching.

Abells, Chana Byers, *The Children We Remember*, Greenwillow Books (New York), 1986. Depicts the lives of Jewish children before the Nazis' rise to power and afterwards.

Adler, David A., *Child of the Warsaw Ghetto*, Holiday House (New York), 1995. A nonfiction picture book biography of Froim Baum, who survived several death camps.

Adler, David A., *Children of the Holocaust*, Hoiday House (New York), 1994. A picture book about two children who were killed in the Holocaust.

Adler, David, *The Number on My Grandfather's Arm*, UAHC Press (New York), 1987. A young girl finds out about the Holocaust from her grandfather when she asks him about the number tattooed on his arm.

Adler, David, *A Picture Book of Jewish Holidays*, Holiday House (New York), 1981. "This book of simple facts is filled with the warmth of the Sabbath, the wonder of Hanukkah, the solemnity of Yom Kippur, the freedom of Passover, the joy of Purim, and more." Grade 1+.

Ayer, Eleanor H., *Exploring Cultures of the World: Poland, a Troubled Past, a New Start*, Benchmark Books (New York), 1996. What is Poland like today, now that the communists are gone? Contains some photographs. Grade 5+.

Bachrach, Susan D., *Tell Them We Remember: The Story of the Holocaust*. Little, Brown and Co. (Boston), 1994. One and a half million of the Holocaust victims were children. Sponsored by the United States Holocaust Memorial Museum, this history of what led to the Holocaust, the Holocaust itself and the aftermath, focuses on individual children of that time. Every page has a photograph from the archives of the museum. A worthwhile book for your school library.

Bernbaum, Israel, *My Brother's Keeper: The Holocaust Through the Eyes of an Artist*, G.P. Putnam's Sons (New York), 1985. This series of five paintings on the Holocaust are called "Warsaw Ghetto 1943." The figures, colors, and situations depicted are symbolic. Each oil painting is shown in full at the beginning of a chapter, and then portions of it are repeated throughout the chapter so that, portion by portion, the symbolism can be explained. Bernbaum urges children of all nations to join hands to declare, "I am my brother's keeper." Grade 5+.

Boas, Jacob, *We Are Witnesses: Five Diaries of Teenagers Who Died in the Holocaust*, Henry Holt and Company (New York), 1995. From Poland, Lithuania, Belgium, Hungary, and the Netherlands, these teens show that though "Hitler could kill millions...he could not destroy the human spirit." Boas has told each teen's story, with liberal quotes from their diaries.

Brown, Gene, *Anne Frank: Child of the Holocaust*, BlackBirch Press (New York), 1991. Anne's story is retold in easy-to-understand language with photos on every page and quotes from her diary in some margins. Compellingly written. Grade 3+.

Bunting, Eve, *Terrible Things: An Allegory of the Holocaust*, Jewish Publication Society (Philadelphia), 1989. A story of forest animals; it can be used to discuss standing up for what you believe is right, the importance of working together, and the roles of bystanders and witnesses.

Chaikin, Mirim, *Menorahs, Mezuzas, and Other Jewish Symbols*, Clarion Books (New York), 1990. From symbolic ideas and acts, to symbols in the home and in worship, Chaikin helps us better understand Jewish culture. Choose some symbols to display in your classroom. Grade 4+.

Cohn, Janice, *The Christmas Menorahs: How a Town Fought Hate*, Albert Whitman (Morton Grove, Illinois), 1995. How a town responded to Neo-Nazi acts of hate towards the Jews in its community.

Drucker, Malka, *The Family Treasury of Jewish Holidays*, Little, Brown and Company (Boston), 1994. Choose a holiday to celebrate with your class (perhaps Yom Hashoah, Holocaust Remembrance Day). Each chapter tells about the reason for celebrating and how it is done. Stories are told, activities are described, and recipies are given. A great, comprehensive book. Grade 1+ (with help from you, the teacher).

Finkelstein, Norman, *Remember Not to Forget: A Memory of the Holocaust*, Franklin Watts (New York), 1985. With woodcut illustrations, the history of the Jews from 70 AD is traced, looking at the way way they were blamed over the centuries for hardships that came to their neighbors. The Jews could not believe at first that they were in danger in Germany. But then came the violence. The book also looks at the end of the war and the beginning of the State of Israel. Grade 2+.

Frank, Anne, *Anne Frank: The Diary of a Young Girl*, Doubleday (Garden City, New York), 1967. This classic volume scarcely needs introduction. Anne's diary was left behind when she was arrested and eventually sent to a concentration camp. It was only years later that, with encouragement from friends, her father, the only family member to survive, decided to publish his daughter's writing. Grade 5+.

Galloz, Christophe and Roberto Innocenti, *Rose Blanche*, Creative Education (Minnesota), 1985. Evocative, double-page paintings illustrate the story of Rose, who doesn't have a clear understanding of what's happening around her. She wonders where a truckload of children is being taken. She follows its tracks to the forest, where she finds the children behind barbed wire. From then on, she brings them food. Grades 5+.

Greene, Carol, *Elie Wiesel: Messenger from the Holocaust*, Childens Press (Chicago), 1986. Wiesel survived the Holocaust and was determined to bear witness and to give testimony of his experiences and observations. He says "Anyone who does not remember betrays [those who died in the Holocaust} again." Grade 4+.

Heale, Jay, *Cultures of the World: Poland*, Marshall Cavendish (New York), 1994. The Polish survive, despite being erased from the world map at leace twice! Your students can examine geography, history, government, economy, the people, lifestyle, religion, festivals, and food. Great photographs. Grade 4+.

Korbonski, Stefan, *The Jews and the Poles in World War II*, Hippocrene Books (New York, 1989). Over 2,000 Poles were executed for helping to save Jews from death, and more than 100,000 Jews were successfully hidden from Nazis by Polish families and churches. Korbonski argues against the perception of Poles as anti-Semites. A teacher's resource (perhaps suitable for older students).

Kubar, Zofia S., *Double Identity: A Memoir*, Hill and Wang (New York), 1989. Zofia removed her star of David armband, stuffed it in her pocket, and continued to the Aryan side of Warsaw, where she survived, masquerading as a Gentile, through sheer wit, audacity, and courage. This book reads like a novel and is suitable for older students.

Leigh, Vanora, *Anne Frank*, Wayland (Hove, England), 1985. Anne's story is retold with photos of her and of the period in which she lived, plus painted illustrations showing scenes from the diary, which add life to the story. Easy to read. Grade 3+.

Matas, Carol, *Daniel's Story*, Scholastic, Inc. (New York), 1993. "Although Daniel is a fictitious character, his story was inspired by the real experiences of many of the more than one million children who died in the Holocaust." This book is published in conjunction with the United States Holocaust Memorial Museum.

Matas, Carol, *Jesper*, Lester and Orpen Dennys (Toronto), 1989. Teenage Jesper and his friends in the Danish resistance put their lives on the line with the Germans constantly at their heels.

Matas, Carol, *Lisa*, Lester and Orpen Dennys (Toronto), 1987. Hitler has invaded Denmark and 12-year-old Jewish Lisa becomes a secret messenger for the Danish resistance.

Meltzer, Milton, *Rescue: The Story of How Gentiles Saved Jews in the Holocaust*, Harper and Row (New York), 1988. This collection of stories calls us "to remember not only the evil done by racism, but also the heroes and heroines whose moral choices and actions show us that one need not be passive or silent in the face of evil." Intermediate.

Niezabitowska, Malgorzata, "Remants: The Last Jews of Poland," *National Geographic*, September 1986. In 1939 Poland was a world center of Jewish culture with nearly 3.5 million Jews living there. Now there remains about 5,000, most of whom are old. This is their story and their lament.

Oppenhein, Shulamith Levey, *The Lily Cupboard*, Charlotte Zolotow, 1992. Little Miriam must leave her parents for safety with a non-Jewish family in rural Holland. When soldiers come looking, she finds safety in a lily cupboard. Easy-reading picture book.

Orgel, Doris, *The Devil in Vienna*, Dial Press (New York), 1978. Two girls are best friends, but when Hitler invades, Lieselotte joins the Hitler Youth and Inge is marked as a Jew. Can their friendship survive? Grade 4+.

Orlev, Uri, *The Man from the Other Side*, Houghton Mifflin (Boston), 1991. Marek lives just outside the Warsaw Ghetto during World War II. He is pressed by his stepfather to help carry food to the Jews through the sewer system. But that is just the beginning. Grade 5+.

Prager, Arthur and Emily Prager, *World War II Resistance Stories*, Franklin Watts (New York), 1979. Five stories are told, including the one about Witold Pilecki who, concerned about imprisoned Poles, purposely gets arrested so that he can be sent to Auschwitz to help the prisoners organize and survive their ordeal. Grade 3+.

Rosenberg, Maxine, *Hiding to Survive: Stories of Children Rescued from the Holocaust*, Clarion Books (New York), 1994. Fourteen first-person accounts, including three from Poland. Grade 4+.

The Spirit That Moves Us: A Literature-Based Resource Guide: Teaching about Diversity, Prejudice, Human Rights, and the Holocaust. For grades K-4: Maine Holocaust Human Rights Center. Available from Tilbury House, Publisher, 800-582-1899. An excellent literature-based curriculum guide and resource. A similar guide for grades 5–8 will be published by Tilbury House in May 1997.

Teaching About the Holocaust: A Resource Guide for Educators, U.S. Holocaust Memorial Museum (Washington). This excellent book, with six artifact photos, is part of a free teacher's packet, available from the U.S. Holocaust Memorial Museum. Call 202-488-2661 to request it.

Thoene, Bodie, *Warsaw Requiem*, Bethany House (Minneapolis), 1991. This is a I-can't-put-it-down novel for older students (grades 7+ and teachers. A myriad of characters from Palenstine through Germany and France to England intertwine their lives as they deal with the evil of the Nazi agenda. The chief setting, however, is Warsaw (May to September, 1941), where the Lubetkin family must balance Orthodox Jewish beliefs with the unforeseen danger of the Nazi invasion. Read this and you'll want to back up and read the previous five books of the Zion Covenent Series

van der Rol, Ruud, and Rian Verhoeven, *Anne Frank: Beyond the Diary, A Photographic Remembrance*, Penguin (New York), 1993. Written in association with the Anne Frank House, the book is crammed with photographs plus a cutaway drawing of the Secret Annex. Grade 4+, although younger children can appreciate the photographs.

Wild, Margaret, *A Time for Toys*, Kids Can Press (Toronto), 1991. Miriam lives in Hut 18, Bed 22. She remembers the toys she had when she lived with Mama and Papa at home. But here, there are no toys. So she and the women are making toys out of scraps they find to celebrate when the soldiers come to free them. Realistic illustrations depict the threadbare conditions of the camp.

Wilkes, Sybella, *One Day We Had to Run*, Milbrook Press (Brookfield, CT), 1995. Refugee children tell their stories in words and paintings.

Wall 7 Divali: Celebrating Renewal

Pre-Reading Warm-Up

1. A Hindu Tradition: Painted Prayers

"Women and children please Lakshmi, the goddess of wealth and prosperity, by sketching peacocks, lotuses, and elephants on their walls with paint made from rice flour and water."

Like the spinning of the prayer wheel in Tibet, the painting of designs and symbols that are believed to please Lakshmi on the walls of houses, fences, floors, and roof-tops in India is a form of prayer aimed at asking for blessings from the deities.

Ask your students about the different ways prayers are said and performed in different faiths and religions. Some examples are: meditating and praying at the fourteen Stations of the Cross, praying with the rosary, taking part in the liturgy of the mass, receiving Holy Communion, making a pilgrimage to Mecca by the Muslims, praying at the Western Wall in Jerusalem by the Jews, burning of incense by many religions, meditation, private and group prayers, hymn singing, and written prayers by Christians.

Ask students to come up with the purposes of praying. Put their answers on the chalkboard. Discuss if it matters what method we choose to pray.

2. Celebrating Holidays

While holidays are celebrated under different names and in different ways, their functions are essentially the same. They serve social, cultural, recreational, and religious purposes at the same time. Holidays unite people—friends, families, and strangers—in the same celebration. This serves to strengthen the bonds of the family and community and to provide recreation, relief from daily routines, and a focus for spiritual and affective belonging.

Ask your students to list the major holidays celebrated in our country. Put their suggestions on the chalkboard. Ask them what these holidays have in common, and what functions they serve.

Language Arts

3. Storytime

The Hindu culture and religion is full of colorful stories that capture the imagination of any age (see "Draupadi: Daughter of Fire!" in Activity # 16, plus the bibliography at the end of this chapter). Select a few stories and read them to your class. While you are reading, they may sketch interpretive drawings which can then be displayed in the classroom.

4. Picture-Inspired Story Writing

The Transcendental Gallery (see Activity #15) is full of wonderful paintings from Hindu mythology. Offer the students an opportunity to view these paintings on screen or, alternatively if you have a color printer, print some of the pictures to post in the classroom for your students to enjoy. Allow each student to select a painting and write a story based on the illustration. Perhaps you could bind the stories and illustrations into a class book to share with parents and visitors during an open house

5. Comparative Religious Stories

Most students have some religious experience though not necessarily the same as each other. Invite the students to share a story or two from their religious heritage, either orally or written. If the students share orally, give the listening students an opportunity to ask questions and for the speaking student to answer. How do the stories differ? How are they the same? Make a chart at the front of the class to facilitate comparisons

Social Studies

6. A Comparative Study of Two Cultures: Indian and Chinese

Divali is the Festival of Lights held each year in honor of the goddess of prosperity, harvest, and fertility, Lakshmi. It is celebrated in autumn between October and November as an end-of-the-year ritual, in preparation for a prosperous new year.

The custom includes cleaning the home from top to bottom, giving the exterior and the interior a new coat of paint. Women decorate the newly painted walls and floor with folk art rich with religious symbols to please Lakshmi, the goddess. The festivities begin in the evening. Candles are burned and colorful lanterns are lit. Family members and friends take part in a festive feast and recreational entertainment afterwards. Gambling is considered to be an activity that would invite prosperity. Doors and windows are opened to invite the goddess Lakshmi to enter the home. Alaksmi, the goddess of bad fortune, is chased out with loud noises made by banging pots and pans and lighting firecrackers.

Chinese New Year, which is celebrated at around the beginning of February, shares very similar customs and beliefs as Divali. As Chinese New Year, also known as the Festival of Spring, is a concerted wish for renewal and prosperity, the home is also cleaned from top to bottom weeks before the festival. Often, a new coat of paint is applied to the home. In preparation for renewal, everybody has a new haircut and a new wardrobe. Special foods are prepared ahead of time for the festivities.

Beginning on New Year's Eve and for the following ten days, firecrackers are lit, folk dances are performed, and good wishes are exchanged. Lucky money is given out to well-wishers. The home is decorated with all sorts of spring motifs, such as cherry blossoms, red scrolls of wishes, plates of fruits.

The god of good fortune and prosperity is welcomed through visits by well-wishers. Ill fortune is expelled from the home by the noise of firecrackers and the vigorous performance of lion and dragon dancers. The floor is not swept for the first three days of the new year for fear that good fortune would be swept away.

Throughout the ten-day celebration, relatives, friends, and neighbors visit. They exchange good wishes, lucky money, and gifts of fresh fruit. A festive feast is held every night where participants party until the late hours. Gambling is also viewed as a window of opportunity for wealth and good fortune.

Discuss with your class the notion of "cultural universals" in which similar cultural traits and customs happen across the cultures. Brainstorm together about the cultural customs we share with people of other lands.

7. Cultural Symbols

Peacocks. lotuses, floral designs, elephants, and pyramids of rice are symbols of good fortune, prosperity, and happiness in the Hindu belief.

Ask your students to brainstorm about the symbols that are significant in their faiths and cultures. Some examples are the cross, the triangle, the dove, the olive branch, and the peace sign. Encourage them to explain why these symbols are held in high regard. Involve their parents in helping out with the meanings if the students do not know them.

The students could illustrate the symbols they have researched and display them in the classroom. They could also create new sumbols for their school, classroom, or family.

Science

8. Elephants

Study the elephant. How do the elephants of Africa and India differ? What habitat do they seek? Have your students research the diet, life span, size, and behavior. Compare tame and wild elephants, their enemies, and the elephant's use by man. (See the bibliography at the end of this chapter for some resources.)

9. Tigers

The tiger is the national animal of India. Each tiger has distinctive face markings that make it possible for people to distinguish one tiger from another. They hunt and kill for food, mark their own territory, and get chased off their food by crocodiles! What else can your students learn about tigers? (See the bibliography at the end of this chapter.)

Mathematics

10. Hindu Population

Compare the size of the Hindu population in India and around the world. Younger students can order the countries from most to least Hindus, using the raw data. Older students can calculate percentage of total population in each country and order that data from greatest to least. Below, listed alphabetically, are those countries whose predominant religion is Hinduism and also those countries studied in this book whose Hindu populations are listed in the source material. (Source: *Encyclopaedia Britannica 1995 Book of the Year*.)

Country	Hindu Population	Total Population
Guyana	249,000	733,000
India	734,000,000	913,744,000
Mauritius	570,000	2,069,000
Nepal	16,829,000	19,525,000
South Africa	440,000	41,749,000
Surinam	116,000	423,000
United Kingdom	410,000	58,422,000
United States	900,000	260,967,000

Arts and Crafts

11. Painted Prayers for Divali

Using Stephen P. Huyler's book, *Painted Prayers: Women's Art in Village India* (from your local public library or inter-library loan program), show your class the rich photographs of the wall and floor paintings by Indian women in India.

Divide your class into groups of five. Provide each group with a long sheet of brown or black art paper that comes in a roll. The dimension of the strip of art paper for each group should be around 3 feet (1 meter) by 9 feet (3 meters). Designate a piece of the hallway wall for each group to hang their paper on with tape.

Provide each group with three ice cream pails and three wooden spoons/paint stirrers. Each group mixes a small amount of all-purpose flour with cold water to make a white solution. A couple of students are designated as flour solution stirrers, while the other three in the group will be painters. Throughout the activity, the stirrers and the painters will exchange jobs at your signals.

Instruct your groups to lightly sketch the Lakshmi and Hindu symbols, such as the peacock, elephant, lotus, and floral designs, on the strip of art paper. Then as the flour solution is being stirred (flour settles to the bottom if undisturbed for a long time), the painters will use their fingers, as Hindu women do, to paint the symbols and design on the dark-colored art paper.

Leave the painted prayers murals up for a week or so as an exhibit of folk art.

12. Making Divali Clay Diyas (Divas)

Divali commemorates the welcome return of Prince Rama and his wife, Sita, after fourteen years of banishment from their homeland. The villagers guided their prince and princess home with candle-lit lamps called diyas (or divas). At Divali, diyas are lit to invite Lakshmi, the goddess of health, wealth, and prosperity to their homes, besides being a remembrance of the adventures of Prince Rama.

Divide your class into pairs. Provide each pair of students with the following:

Materials:

>Old cutting board
>Rolling pin
>Self-hardening clay, such as Playdoh
>Modelling tool with a flat edge
>Water-based liquid tempera paint of various colors
>Paint brush, round and size 8 or 10
>Tea candle on an metal base (obtainable in crafts stores and some grocery stores)

Method:

1. Roll out the clay so that it is about 1/2" (1 cm) thick. Using the modelling tool, mark out a leaf shape at least 1/2" (1 cm) larger than the circumference of the fat candle. Cut out the shape with the tool.
2. Shape the diya in the hand so that it has a slightly raised edge and tapers at one end. Designs can be edged into the clay with the tool.
3. Leave the diya to dry overnight.
4. On the following day, using the liquid tempera paint, decorate the diya with painted patterns.
5. When dry, place the fat, stubby tea candle with its metal base in the diya. The Divali diya is complete.
6. As lit candles are dangerous, do not let your students light them indoors. It's safer to take your class outdoors to light the diyas on the playground.

Food Experience

13. Recipe

Divali celebrates the homecoming of Prince Rama and Sita after they had conquered evil in the form of the buffalo-headed Mahishasura. It is, in effect, a celebration of victory over evil. The festival is a time for family reunion. Women indulge in making all kinds of sweets, while children enjoy playing with sparklers and small fireworks. One of India's most delicious and nutritious desserts is Gajar Halwa.

Gajar Halwa

Ingredients:

>14 ounces water
>14 ounces sweetened condensed milk (not evaporated)
>2 cups grated carrot
>1 cup cooking oil, butter, or margarine
>2 tablespoons each chopped blanched almonds and raisins

1/4 teaspoon ground saffron (if this is hard to find, use 2 or 3 drops of yellow food coloring)
1 tablespoon fresh lime juice, heated

Method:
1. Soak saffron in heated lime juice.
2. Place water and condensed milk into a saucepan and bring to a boil.
3. Add carrot and cook over low heat about 45 minutes, stirring occasionally.
4. Add oil gradually.
5. Cook until fat begins to separate.
6. Stir in almonds, raisins, saffron, and lime juice. May be eaten hot or cold.

Internet Resources

14. A Divali Ritual

Carrie Carolin, not a Hindu herself, presents an Americanized version of Divali ritual which she practices each year. She begins her description of the ritual with this disclaimer, "Absolutely no flaming about this ritual will be tolerated or paid attention to—nor will I do anything more than laugh at any e-mail from Christians telling me this ritual is Satanic, because it is NOT!" To learn more, go to:
URL: *http://www.cascade.net/laksmi.html*

You will find here:
*   Who is Laksmi? (photo included);
*   What is the Laksmi Divali Festival? (another photo of Laksmi);
*   A Divali Ritual (still another photo of Laksmi).

15. Transcendental Gallery

The Transcendental Gallery contains a "lush collection of Transcendental Art" which is truly beautiful and which offers a glimpse into the Hindu religion and culture. Each of the more than 80 paintings is accompanied by commentary. To feast your eyes go to:
URL: *http://www.goloka.com/html/picidx.html*

16. Draupadi: Daughter of Fire!

This is the story of a woman, part goddess, who from birth had wonderful prophecies made about her. Protected by Krishna, she in turn protected another from being cursed. In the end she became the goddess of fortune in the heavenly planet. For a more complete version of her story go to:
URL: *http://www.goloka.com/html/draupad.html*
Stories included are:
*   Wife of the Pandavas
*   Shiva's blessings;
*   The birth of Draupadi to the King of Pancala;
*   The marriage of Draupadi;
*   The Shaming of Draupadi.

Bibliography

Arden, Harvey, "Searching for India: Along the Grand Trunk Road," *National Geographic*, May 1990. India is a country of diversity. Learn more about this subcontinent as you follow the road from Calcutta to Amritsar near the Punjab/Pakistan border.

Bahree, Patricia, *The Hindu World*, Simon and Schuster (New York), 1990. Hinduism is the world's third largest religion. How many gods and goddesses are there? What is family life like? What is it like growing up Hindu? Grade 5+.

Breeden, Stanley, "Tiger! Lord of the Indian Jungle," *National Geographic*, December 1984. For 10 years the authors studied the tigers of two parks in India, using elephants whom the tigers seem to tolerate even with a load of humans on top. The map included show the decreased range of tigers throughout Asia.

Chadwick, Douglas H., "Out of Time, Out of Space: Elephants," *National Geographic*, May 1991. Elephants need a lot of room to live, and man is their chief competitor. Chadwick looks at the beauty of the beast and the declining numbers.

Cumming, David, *Our Country: India*, Wayland (Hove, England), 1990. Features boxed comments from children who live in India, accompanied by a photograph of each child in his/her "natural habitat." Grade 2+.

"The East," *Disney's Wonderful World of Knowledge, Volume 11: Holidays Around the World*. Danbury Press (Danbury, Connecticut), 1973. Two photographs of Divali celebration: one with women holding sparklers in the night and a full-page color photograph of a woman and her colorful floor painting. Page 78 also has a description of Indian holidays and two photographs of celebration.

"Elephants," *The Young Children's Encyclopedia, Volume 5*. Encyclopaedia Britannica Inc. (Chicago), 1977. Learn about elephants and how, in India, even elephants go to school!

"Festival of Lights," *Childcraft: The How and Why Library, Volume 9: Holidays and Customs*. Field Enterprises (Chicago), 1975. A short article about Divali, but a full-page color photograph of a young girl lighting Divali candles. In the same volume, "Pictures on the Ground" briefly describes how the Divali floor paintings are done (black and white photo included).

Hermes, Judith, *The Children of India*, Carolrhoda Publications (New York), 1993. Color photographs and information. Part of "The World's Children" series.

Husain, Shakrukh, *Demons, Gods, and Holy Men from Indian Legends*, Peter Bedrick Books (New York), 1987. Full of wonderful stories, the book includes "Lakshmi, Goddess of Love, Luck, and Wealth." Illustrated. Grade 4+.

Huyler, Stephen P., *Painted Prayers: Women's Art in Village India*. Rizzoli (New York), 1994. Women in India seem to love painting. For some it is a daily ritual; others paint to celebrate special dieties like Lakshmi. More than 170 full-color photographs will help to make this special artwork come alive.

"India," *The Young Children's Encyclopedia, Volume 8*. Encyclopaedia Britannica, Inc. (Chicago), 1977. The Martin family travels through India; a "Where Am I" puzzle, and more detail about India are articles for this entry.

Kadodwala, Dilip, *Hinduism*, Wayland (Hove, England), 1995. Well-illustrated, each page has a wide margin with brief explanations of the larger text or illustrations. Divali is explained, with a photo of some delicious sweets to be shared during the festival. Grade 3+.

Kalman, Bobbie, *India: The Culture*, Crabtree Publishing (New York), 1990. Includes many photographs showing distinctly Indian people, buildings, shrines, art, and activities. "Flavors of India" at the end of the book featuers Indian ice cream and chapates recipes, mealtime manners, spice information, and more. Graded 4+.

Kalman, Bobbie, *India: The Land*, Crabtree Publishing (New York), 1990. India contains mountains, valleys, deserts, and tropics. See the villiages and cities, the farms, markets, and industries, as well as transportation, development, and animals. Grade 4+.

Kalman, Bobbie, *India: The People*, Crabtree Publishing (New York), 1990. How do the people, living so diversely, live in harmony? What is family life like? How do the poor cope? Grade 4+.

Lewin, Ted, *Sacred River*, Clarion Books (New York), 1995. For Hindus, the Ganges is the most sacred river of all. The Ganges flows through Benares, a city in India where many Hindus go for a special pilgrimage.

Lye, Keith, *Take a Trip to India*, Franklin Watts (New York), 1982. An informational book with color photographs. Grades 1+.

McCarry, John, "Bombay: India's Capital of Hope," *National Geographic*, March 1995. Bombay is the richest and most peaceful city in India. Take a glimpse of what life is like there.

McNair, Sylvia, *Enchantment of the World: India*, Childrens Press (Chicago), 1990. Well-illustrated with photographs, the book begins with ancient India and traces her history while looking at the people and their lifestyles. Grade 5+.

Miller, Peter, "Kerala: Jewel of India's Malabar Coast," *National Geographic*, May 1988. Kerala is one of India's smallest states, but the streets are cleaner, health standards are higher, slums are fewer, and the literacy rate is higher than in the rest of India. Miller looks at what makes this corner of India so different. Great pictures.

Mitter, Swasti, *Hindu Festivals*, Rourke Enterprises (Vero Beach, Florida), 1989. Different places celebrate Divali differently. See how it is done in West Bengal, Maharashtra, Punjab, and Giyerat. Other festivals are also described. Grade 4+.

Posell, Elsa, "Elephants," *I Want to Know About..., Volume 19.* Children's Press (Chicago), 1972. Beginning readers can learn where elephants come from, how many kinds there are, what they are like, what they eat, how they live, their enemies, and their capture and taming for the use of man.

"Save the Elephants," *Disney's Wonderful World of Knowledge Yearbook 1991.* Grolier (Danbury, Connecticut), 1991. The elephant is endangered. Why? What are concerned countries doing? Also includes information on diet, size, and differences between African and Indian elephants.

Srinivasan, Radhika, *Cultures of the World: India*, Marshall Cavendish (New York), 1990. Twenty-five states and seventeen official languages! That's just the beginning of the orderly chaos that is India. Grade 5+.

Theroux, Paul, "By Rail Across the Indian Subcontinent," *National Geographic*, June 1984. Built by the British, the "railway is an indispensable fixture of Indian life, carrying 3.7 billion passengers a year." View, through photographs, the scenery, the people, and the life on the train. A history of the railway concludes the article.

Vesilind, Priit J., "Life Breath of Half the World: Monsoons," *National Geographic*, December 1984. The peak season average rainfall in Cherrapunji, India, is 300 inches (762 cm)! Though other countries also experience monsoons, India's experience is the worst.

Ward, Geoffrey C., "India's Wildlife Dilemma," *National Geographic*, May 1992. The animals need the land to survive, but so do the people. "With 2 percent of the world's land and 16 percent of its people, India is fast losing its wildlife habitat."

Wall 8 Ndebele: A Proud and Artistic People

Pre-Reading Warm-Up

1. *National Geographic* and the Ndebele People

Use the wonderful pictorial resource of *National Geographic* magazine (February 1986) to illustrate and introduce the Ndebele people to your class. The younger children will enjoy the photographs (warning: one page shows bare-breasted women), and the older students will find the story informative.

Language Arts

2. Story Time

Read, and/or provide for the class to read, stories that portray the vastneess of the African Continent. See the bibliography at the end of this chapter for some suggestions.

3. Letter Writing

Encourage your students to write for information about the Ndebele people and their art. The following addresses are provided for this purpose.

In South Africa

South African Tourism Board,
442 Rigel Avenue South,
Erasmus-rand 0181,
Private Bag X164, Pretoria 0001
South Africa
Ph. (12) 347-0600

In Zimbabwe

Zimbabwe Tourist Development Corporation,
P.O.B. 8052, Causeway,
Harare
Zimbabwe

In the USA

Embassy of the Republic of South Africa,
3051 Massachusetts Avenue, NW,
Washington, DC 20008
USA
Ph. (202) 265-1607
Fax (202) 232-4400

Embassy of the Republic of Zimbabwe,
2852 McGill Terrace, NW
Washington, DC 20008
USA

In Canada

High Commission for the Republic of
   South Africa,
15 Sussex Drive,
Ottawa, Ontario
Canada
K1M 1M8
Ph. (613) 744-0330
Fax (613) 741-1639

High Commission for the Republic of Zimbabwe,
332 Somerset Street West,
Ottawa, Ontario
Canada
K2P 0J9

4. Journal Writing

After having read the page on Ndebele house painting in *Talking Walls: The Stories Continue*, and the *National Geographic* article (see Activity #1 of this chapter), suggest that your students pretend they are visiting a Ndebele village in South Africa, being hosted by a local family.

Assign students to write a series of at least six daily journal entries, recording the sights, sounds, and simulated personal experiences. (The resources in the bibliography can help with this.)

Social Studies

5. Gender Roles in Society: A Discussion in Context

"For the past three generations, many Ndebele women in South Africa have been painting the walls of their homes.... Many young Ndebele girls look forward to learning how to paint walls from their mothers."

Amazingly similar in the artistic expressions of their respective cultures, women in both rural India and Ndebele in South Africa play a critical role. Women in both cultures are given the important responsibility of passing cultural messages, in the form of folk art, from one generation to another.

Explore with your class what roles are still gender-specific and what others are no longer bound by this bias. List them on the chalkboard in two columns. Discuss the pros and cons of the gradual dissolution of traditional roles based on gender differences. Lead a discussion on how the next generation might be different from ours in the areas of child-rearing, nurturing, education, careers, and social roles.

6. Social Studies: An Action Research

Organize a school-bus tour of your community/city to discover homes, public buildings, and structures that have been beautified with artwork. (This could also be done as individual assignments.) Photograph the painted or sculpted artwork on color slides. Ask your students to notate the locations, with descriptions of the buildings/structures and artwork on notepads.

Back in the classroom, organize the material in the form of a script. When the slides are developed, assist the students in developing a scripted slide show on decorated buildings in your community. They might enjoy choosing and playing an unobtrusive piece of background music to complement the commentary of the show.

7. Geography of Africa: A Hands-On Integrated Learning Activity

The Ndebele people live in two African countries: Zimbabwe and South Africa. The South African Ndebele group lives in their homeland of KwaNdebele ("The Place of the Ndebele"), which is situated in the Eastern Transvaal Highveld to the northeast of Pretoria. The painted houses that decorate the Transvaal Highveld with their distinctive designs announce loudly: "This is an Ndebele home!" The following hands-on activity helps students to quickly learn the countries in the continent of Africa and their locations on the map.

A) Provide each student with color felt-tip markers, an 8 1/2 x 11" (22cm x 30cm) up-to-date outline map of Africa with political boundaries of countries, and a piece of identical-sized cardboard. Ask each student to color the countries of the Continent of Africa so that each country bears a different color. If the countries are not already labelled with their names, students should label them with the help of an atlas or a wall map of Africa.

B) Using glue sticks, students affix their colored and labelled maps onto the cardboard pieces provided. Allow the mounted maps to dry overnight.

C) On the following day, provide your students with sharp blades (e.g., x-acto knives) with which they carefully cut out the outlines of the continent first, then the individual countries, creating jigsaw puzzle maps. Ask students to press hard with the blades so that they cut cleanly. (You might like to invite parents to assist younger students due to the potential hazard of using sharp blades.)

D) Encourage students to become familiar with the shape and location of each African country by assembling their map puzzles. Ask them to exchange map puzzles with each other for a second experience in assembling them.

E) Next, pair up your students. One student will be the observer while the other attempts to assemble the map puzzle blindfolded. The observer may help with giving clues until the puzzle is successfully assembled. The students then trade roles. By the time this activity is performed several times, your students will have become familiar with the countries that make up the continent of Africa. Ask them to place a star on the map of South Africa to indicate where Pretoria is. They will have a pretty good idea where the Ndebele people live—in the southwest of Zimbabwe and to the northeast of Pretoria in South Africa.

8. Apartheid

Apartheid was a policy of the South African government to isolate blacks from whites, giving them nominal independence in arbitrarily formed homelands. Blacks were required to carry passbooks that indicated where each was allowed to travel or work outside of their "homelands." In April 1994 the African National Congress (ANC), headed by Nelson Mandela (see *Talking Walls*; Tilbury House, 1992), won two-thirds of the vote in South Africa's first one-person, one-vote election. Apartheid policy had ended. Assign your students to research the events leading up to this peaceful change in government. (Encyclopedic yearbooks are one good resource for this.)

9. Segregation of People Groups

Compare the policies of apartheid in South Africa with segregation of blacks in the United States and the formation of reservations for native peoples across North America. Compare and contrast:

A) The response of the people isolated;
B) Societal problems created or exacerbated as a result;
C) Solutions that have been attempted (whether or not they succeeded);
D) The lifestyle of the segregated peoples as opposed to that of the majority population;
E) The ability of each group to maintain its traditional culture; and
F) How each group has adjusted to the changes imposed upon them.

Science

10. Big Game of South Africa

Big game stalks the parks of South Africa, protected by laws that keep even traditional hunters away. Lions, elephants, leopards, cheetah, rhinos, zebra, and more all call South Africa home. Each student can choose an individual animal to study. Older students can also compare the present range of habitat with the range of 200-300 years ago. Ask the students to explain the discrepancy. One resource is "A Place for Parks in the New South Africa," listed in the bibliography at the end of this chapter.

11. The Ostrich

The ostrich is a favorite food of South Africa. Even in North America, ostrich farms have begun to spring up. As a class, study the ostrich. What is it? What makes this bird so unique? What would a farmer who chooses to raise ostrich, need for successful husbandry? If there is an ostrich farm near you, by all means visit it. Besides meat, what other uses has mankind of the ostrich (feathers, eggs etc.)? What is the size of the ostrich egg? Compare it, by weight to a chicken egg. How many people would need to come to breakfast if you served ostrich egg omelet as the main course?

Mathematics

12. Patterning

Have the students choose (or you may choose for them) a design from Ndebele paintings (there are plenty to choose from amongst the *National Geographic* magazines and the Internet sites listed below), and continue the pattern. For instance, the large rectangular block in the center of the Ndebele picture in *Talking Walls: The Stories Continue* could be continued in a pattern either vertically or horizontally. Other portions of that same painted wall could also be extended in patterns. This helps younger (and not so young) children develop problem-solving skills.

Arts and Crafts

13. Communicating with Art: A Study of Folk Art

"Some women paint to celebrate a son's passage into manhood. Others say they decorate their walls to honor their ancestors, while still others say that the patterns are purely for decoration."

All cultures, past and present, communicate their cultural identities through arts and crafts. The ancient Maya painted their history on walls. Indian and Ndebele women paint their houses and floors. The indigenous peoples of the Americas are rich with their cultural artifacts, from soapstone carvings, totem poles, and cedar houses, to hide decorations. East Asians, for centuries, have been building and decorating their temples of worship.

Ask groups of five students to brainstorm and research cooperatively art forms that are/were used to communicate the cultural identities of populations around the world today and in the past. Provide three days for their cooperative work. Each group could submit its findings in writing as well as in an oral presentation in class. Encourage students to use pictures, slides, and other kinds of graphics to illustrate their discoveries.

14. Mural Painting: An Arts and Crafts Activity

The design and color brilliancy of the artwork produced by the women of India and Ndebele, the Pueblo of New Mexico, and the Navajo of Arizona bear close resemblance. Invite an art curator or an art professor to talk about the similarities and differences of these forms of folk art. Your students would benefit from seeing a display of art samples.

Following the guest lecture, provide students with an opportunity to express their own cultural messages through an activity in producing pop art on a long strip of art paper (3 feet by 9 feet) taped to the hallway adjacent to your classroom. Provided with water-soluble tempera paint and paint brushes, each student draws a design on the "mural" sheet. This exercise may be done in conjunction with the learning activities suggested for the chapter on the Anti-Graffiti Network in Philadelphia.

Food Experience

15. Recipe

"A typical meal for Ndebele consists of a thick porridge made from maize, complemented with sour milk and wild green vegetables. Other common foods include cornmeal stew, roasted turtle steaks, raw hens' eggs, caterpillars and insects, and sun-dried, salt-cured, or freshly slaughtered raw meats. Monkey meat, which is eaten by some African cultures, is forbidden by Ndebele custom." (from Internet site *http://danenet.wicip.org/mmsd-cso/west/africa.htm*)

Biltong is a popular dried meat eaten in South Africa. The following recipe comes straight from Greg Nietsky, manager of Babblers Restaurant in Roodepoort, Guateng, South Africa (near Johannesburg). Mr. Nietsky has graciously added several recipes to his restaurant home page, including photographs. To access go to;

Biltong

Ingredients:

(The metric measurements are the more accurate)
11 pounds (5 kg) beef fillet, rump or sirloin
1/2 pound (.25 kg) fine salt
3 tablespoons (50 ml) brown sugar
2 teaspoons (10 ml) baking soda
3/4 teaspoon (4 ml) saltpeter
1 teaspoon (5 ml) pepper
3/4 ounce (100 g) coarsely ground coriander
vinegar
7 tablespoons (100 ml) vinegar mixed with 1 quart (1 liter) warm water

Method:

1. Cut meat into strips 2 to 2-3/4 inches (5 to 7 cm) thick, with some fat on each strip.
2. Mix salt, sugar, soda, saltpeter, pepper and coriander and rub into meat.
3. Layer meat, larger pieces first, in a container (not iron), sprinkling a little vinegar over each layer.
4. Leave in a cool place for 24 to 48 hours, depending on how thick the meat is and how salty you want the biltong to be.
5. Dip biltong in vinegar and water mixture to make it shiny and dark.
6. Pat dry and attach hooks or pieces of string.
7. Hang in a cool, dry airy place (try a school storeroom).
8. Biltong should be about 2 inches (5 cm) apart, so that air can circulate freely around pieces.
9. Leave for 2 to 3 weeks, depending on how tender meat is.
(Makes about 4-1/2 pounds (2 kg) of biltong.)

Because of the preservative qualities of saltpeter and vinegar, there is no danger of the meat turning rancid even though it is left out at room temperature (preferably a bit cooler). Saltpeter is available from your pharmacist. Once made, the biltong can last years (almost) and never turn bad.

Internet Resources

16. Postcards from South Africa

This site is really a commercial one, hoping to sell postcards. However, the photographs are so very informative of the Ndebele artwork, that it would be a pity to miss it. Go to:
URL: *http://mail.icon.co.za/~jdiginews/postcard.htm*

Photos included are:

- Ndebele girl with traditional beaded leg hoops;
- Ostrich egg painted;
- A man with traditional ceremonial headdress;
- Outside wall surrounding a kitchen window;
- Ndebele girl in ceremonial dress
- Painted walls;
- Two brothers in front of a colorful house.

17. Traditional African Societies

To read short descriptions of some traditional African societies and see some photographs, go to:
URL: *http://danenet.wicip.org/mmsd-cso/west/africa.htm*

Societies discussed are:
- Masai;
- Dinka
- Malinke
- Wolof;
- Zulu;
- Ndebele.

("Society" is a word some anthropologists use instead "tribe.")

Bibliography

"Africa," *The Young Children's Encyclopedia, Volume 1*. Encyclopaedia Britannica Inc. (Chicago), 1977. Three articles about Africa are here: 1) Not much used to change in African villages. Then school was introduced. Read how that changed things. 2) Amos Biwott, from Kenya, wins the Olympic gold medal for running, and his village folk now feel part of the larger world. 3) More about Africa.

Aardema, Verna, *Why Mosquitos Buzz in People's Ear: A West African Tale*, Dial Press (New York), 1975. An amusing story, it has become a children's classic. Grade 1+. Aardema has written many, many more African tales. Look for *Bimwil and the Zimwi: A Tale from Zanzibar; Who's in Rabbit's House: A Masai Tale; Bringing the Rain to Kapiti Plain; Tales from the Story Hat, Princess Gorilla and New Kind of Water: A Mpongwe Tale; Tales for the Third Ear: From Equatorial Africa and Behind the Back of the Mountain; Black Folktales from Southern Africa*; plus many more.

Asare, Nana, "The Adventures of Coalpot," *Childcraft: The How and Why Library, Volume 3: Children Everywhere*. Field Enterprises (Chicago), 1975. A story from Ghana. Claystove is alarmed that Mame Nyame, the woman who uses Claystove for cooking, has bought a coal pot to do her cooking on now. Coalpot doesn't want to be a competitor, though, and acknowledges Claystove as the mistress of the kitchen. But what happens when Mame Nyame decides to buy an electric stove?

Ayo, Yvonne, *Eyewitness Books: Africa*, Stoddart (Toronto), 1995. All Eyewitness Books are glorious to the eye, each page crammed with illustrations. In this book, you can compare dwellings from different regions, examine self adornment and attire, and learn about beliefs, myths, and magic—from Morocco in the north, to South Africa. Grade 2+.

"The Biggest Bird in the World," *The Young Children's Encyclopedia, Volume 11*. Encyclopaedia Britannica Inc. (Chicago), 1977. Why does the ostrich bury its head? How does it defend itself? Can it fly? This article will help younger children with the science activity on ostriches.

Chadwick, Douglas H., "A Place for Parks in the New South Africa," *National Geographic*, July 1996. South Africa has a number of National Parks to preserve wildlife. Lions, elephants, leopards, rhinos, and zebras thrive there; but will the increasing needs of legitimate social concern drain the money needed to maintain the parks?

Fisher, Angel, "A Continent Speaks Through its Decorative Art: Africa Adorned," *National Geographic*, November 1984. Methods of decorating oneself have been used across Africa. Come, feast your eyes on the art of a continent. (Note: some scenes of partial nudity.)

Georges, D.V., *A New True Book: Africa*, Childrens Press (Chicago), 1986. Very easy reading with large print, pictures, and a map. Grade 1+.

Ibongia, John M. and M. Dobrin, "The Magic Stone," *Childcraft: The How and Why Library, Volume 3: Children Everywhere*. Field Enterprises (Chicago), 1975. A story from Kenya. Grandma tells a story—to the grandchildren who share her hut—about two brothers, one rich and greedy, and the other poor and needy.

Jeffrey, David, "Ndebele People: Pioneers in Their Own Land," *National Geographic*, February 1986. This article describes life in KwaNdebele, an arbitrarily formed "homeland" for the Ndebele people created by apartheid policy. Through photos, see the colorful paintings, traditional attire, and the poverty. A map of South Africa shows the location of KwaNdebele and the other black "homelands."

Laade, Wolfgang, *Music of Man Archive: Zimbabwe, The Ndebele People*. Jecklin Musikhaus (Zurich), 1991. Laade has gone among the Ndebele of Zimbabwe (whom he says are quite a different people group from those in South Africa) and recorded the music of childhood and other stages of life, as well as the music for work, war, and dancing. One compact disc and a 64-page booklet (with words, translations, and information about the culture) included.

Legassick, Martin, "World Affairs: South Africa," *Encyclopaedia Britannica 1995 Book of the Year*. A report on the change in government and the events of the months directly before and after the inauguration of President Nelson Mandela.

Murray, Jocelyn, *Cultural Atlas for Young People: Africa*, Facts on File (New York), 1990. This book is divided into two parts. The "History of Africa" covers geography, explorers, ancient kingdoms, slave trade, religions, and peoples. The "Regional Guide" looks at nomadic life, North Africa, Great Zimbabwe, Southern African, hunter gatherers of Southern Africa, and all of the places in between. Grades 4+.

Onadipe, Kola, "The Flight from Home," *Childcraft: The How and Why Library Volume 3: Children Everywhere*. Field Enterprises (Chicago), 1975. A tale from Nigeria. "This story takes place in a West African village so tiny it cannot be found on a map. But the story gives an idea of what life is like in the many such villages in Africa."

Rosmarin, Ike, *Cultures of the World: South Africa*, Marshall Cavendish (New York), 1993. Though no special mention of the Ndebele people is made, the book gives a panorama of the country, contrasting the lifestyle differences between the blacks and whites. Grade 4+.

Wall 9 The Dog Wall: A Monument to Dogged Loyalty

Pre-Reading Warm-Up

1. Cultural Symbols

The dog wall at Shibuya Station in Tokyo is a silent yet loud testimony to the loyalty and faithfulness of Akita dogs in Japan as represented by Hachiko and his incredible story. Throughout history, we have identified significant universal values and noble characteristics which we uphold and to which we aspire, such as loyalty, courage, and determination, to name just a few.

Ask your students to brainstorm about symbols important to their lives and to the lives of others. The American bald-headed eagle, the Canadian beaver, the British lion and unicorn, the Chinese dragon, the Swiss cross, the French fleur-de-lys, the Christian cross, the Islamic moon, the Jewish Star of David, and the Russian bear are some examples.

Assign to each student a cultural symbol as a research topic. A drawing of the symbol and a description of the symbolic significance are the components of the activity. When the assignment is complete, bind the researched symbols together to become the *Book of Cultural Symbols* of your class.

Language Arts

2. Incredible Animal Stories

The story of Hachiko, the legendary faithful dog, added to our collection of stories of animal valor and loyalty around the world. Read another story about animal loyalty/faithfulness to your class. Assign them two writing assignments:

A) Ask your students identify, locate, and read stories of outstanding loyalty and courage displayed by animals towards people. Ask them to rewrite those stories in their own words and illustrate them. Provide an opportunity for your students to read their stories to the class.

B) Assign students to create their own real or fictional stories about extraordinary animals.

3. Biographical Study

Often, a person who is renowned for one event is somehow related with another. Helen Keller is such a person. She was credited with bringing the first Akita dog to the United States. On her lecture tours to Japan in 1937, her appreciative hosts in Akita City presented Helen Keller with an Akita puppy. Unfortunately, the puppy died several months later after they had returned to New York. A second Akita was sent to Helen Keller from her Japanese friends. Thus began the introduction of the exotic Akita breed to America.

Helen Keller herself is an example of wisdom, patience, and faithfulness. Select a biography of Helen Keller as a class reader.

4. Creative Paragraph Writing

Ask your students to write a paragraph or more, in the first person account (students pretend that they are Hachiko), of what might have gone through the dog's mind when his master failed to come home on that fateful day, May 21, 1925. They might like to draw a picture to go along with this.

5. Letter Writing

Ask your students to write to one of the following addresses for more information about Japan's most favored breed of dog, the Akita.

In Japan

Department of Tourism
2-1-3 Kasumigaseki,
Chiyoda-ku, Tokyo 100
Japan
Ph. (3) 3580-4488; Fax (3) 3580-7901

In the U.S.

Embassy of Japan
2520 Massachusetts Avenue, NW
Washington, DC 20008 -2869
USA
Ph. (202) 939-6700; Fax (202) 328-2187

In Canada

Embassy of Japan
255 Sussex Drive
Ottawa, Ontario
Canada
K1N 9E6
Ph. (613) 241-8541; Fax (613) 241-2232

Social Studies

6. Map Reading

Find a map of Tokyo (*Britannica Atlas* is one source) and have your students locate the Shibuya suburb.

7. Identifying and Making Models of Local Monuments

"In Tokyo at the Shibuya Train Station, Japanese teens often tell their friends to meet them at the 'Dog Wall.' "

The imposing figure of the world-renowned faithful dog is sculptured in bronze and erected on a huge granite block for all Tokyo commuters to see as they pass through the Shibuya train station. Explore with your class the popular landmarks (statues, monuments, buildings, walls, etc.) which are used by people as meeting places in your community.

As a social studies project, assign your students to identify the major landmarks/monuments erected in your community. They will research the social and historical significance of at least two monuments of their choice. As an active learning activity of the project, the students could be asked to make scale models of the monuments with cardboard, papier maché, or a flour-sawdust mixture. (Please refer to "Teacher's Notes" at the back of this chapter for the ingredients and method in making this sculpting medium, or Activity #12 in Part I of this *Teacher's Guide* for a recipe for papier mâché.)

Science

8. Trains

The young and the not-so-young love trains: how they work, what they look like, the intricate operations of signals and switches, etc. The Dog Wall is at a train station. If you teach younger children, set up a train set in your classroom, making it as elaborate as your budget or temporary loans will allow. (Brio, Lego, and Playmobile all make child-friendly train sets.) Label as many parts of the train, tracks, and system as the detail of the system will allow. To extend this activity to art, allow the students to create props out of paper, clay, or whatever else is at hand. Perhaps they could even make a Dog Wall to put at their miniature station.

Older students can research more carefully the different types of trains: subways, monorail, elevated trains, rapid transit, passenger, freight, bullet, etc. They should be able to show, with diagrams and words, the differences in each kind and what the best use of each is. What is the latest train technology? What kind of trains are used in Japan? in Tokyo?

9. Dog Breeds

Study dogs: their breeds, their usefulness to man, and their skills. (See the bibliography at the end of this chapter for some resources.)

10. Save Endangered Species

"We didn't inherit the earth from our ancestors.
We borrowed it from our descendants." (Anonymous)

Between the 17th century and 1927 (when Akita preservation efforts began in Japan), the breed suffered near extinction several times. The sentimental story of Hachiko, which began in 1925, awakened people around the world to make a concerted effort in conserving the near-extinct Akita and preserve the purity of its breed.

Lead your class in identifying the endangered animal species around the world today. Brainstorm ways in which we can do something to preserve the continuation of those species. Do the same with endangered plant species. As a cooperative project, guide your class in publishing a book entitled "Endangered Species, Endangered World."

When the project is complete, send copies of your class project to classes of the same grade in your neighborhood schools and challenge them to embark on a community effort in preserving endangered species around the world. If your school has Internet resources, start up a class/school home page and alert students and adults around the world to the urgency and importance of a global effort to save our endangered plants and animals.

Mathematics

11. Population Comparison

The population of metropolitan Tokyo is roughly 12,000,000 people. How does this compare with the population of your community, county, or state? Provide the students with the statistics for your community and ask them whether they need to divide or multiply the numbers you provide to reach 12 million. How many of your communities could fit into Tokyo in terms of population?

For younger students, simplify the numbers to fit their abilities. For example, 12 million and 12 apples have a similarity: they are both 12 something. If your community population is, say, 1 million, the numbers the students work with can be 12 and 1 rather than 12,000,000 and 1,000,000. If you live in a very small community, instead of providing numbers for your young students, provide counters in proportion to the populations you are studying: one color for your town and another for Tokyo. Ask them to estimate (by counting the counters) how many people live in Tokyo for every person who lives in your community.

Look at the area of your community (square miles or km). Metropolitan Tokyo covers an area of 827 square miles (2,141 square km). How many times would your community fit into Tokyo in terms of area? Is there a difference between this number and the one for population? See if your students can answer this. Introduce the concept of population density and have them calculate the density of your community and that of Tokyo. (Statistics from *Encylopaedia Britannica 1994 Year Book* and *Encyclopaedia Britannica Micropaedia Volume X, 15th edition.*)

Arts and Crafts

12. Akita Dog Modelmaking

Using a photo or illustration of an Akita from a book about dog breeds, help students make statuettes of the dog with papier maché or a flour-and-sawdust sculpting medium. (Please refer to the ingredients and method contained in "Teacher's Notes" towards the end of this chapter and or Activity #12 in Part I of this *Teacher's Guide*.)

When the products are dry in two days' time, provide your students with water-soluble tempera paint and #10 round paint brushes to color their Akita statuettes.

Food Experience

13. Recipes

Many Japanese eat this soup every morning, changing the vegetables according to the season. Miso paste is available at most Oriental food stores and comes in a variety of types. *Shiro-miso* is mild and low in salt. *Aka-miso* is very salty and has a stronger flavor. *Dashi* is the fish stock on which miso soup is based and can also be purchased at Asian grocers. Great variety is possible with this soup, and the recipe below should be considered as a guideline only; your students may prefer different vegetables.

Miso Soup
Ingredients:

> 30 1/2-inch cubes tofu
> 4 mushrooms
> 2 stalks green onions, chopped
> 4 cups water
> 2 teaspoons *dashi*
> 3-4 tablespoons *miso* (adjust to taste)

Method:

1. Bring to a boil 4 cups of water and *dashi*.
2. Add tofu and mushrooms and simmer on low heat for 3 minutes. (If desired, substitute vegetables from the list below. Those with an asterisk (*) should cook longer, for about 10 minutes.)
3. Add *miso* and dissolve completely.
4. Turn off heat immediately. (The *miso* flavor will be lost if you overcook it.)
5. Add chopped green onions.
6. Serve hot.

Note: The following vegetables, etc. can be used instead of, or in addition to, the mushrooms and tofu:

> Chinese cabbage, cut into bite-size squares or triangles
> Cabbage, cut into bite-size squares or triangles
> Lettuce, cut into bite-size squares or triangles.
> Green onions, sliced
> Onions, sliced
> Leeks, sliced or chopped
> Okra, chopped
> Butternut squash*, thinly sliced
> Snow pea pods
> Green beans*
> Daikon*, thinly sliced
> Sweet potatoes*, thinly sliced
> Mushrooms, sliced

Bean sprouts
Tofu, cut into small cubes
Wakame seaweed
Natto beans, minced green pepper, and celery are not recommended.

Internet Resources

14. Kids' Space

Kids' Space is an Internet site out of Japan, a place for primary school kids to communicate with other kids from Japan and around the world. Students may send their drawings, stories, etc. to the site, and may look at what other kids and classes have done. This is also a place where your students have a chance to make e-mail penpals. Go to:
URL: *http://plaza.interport.net/kids_space/guide/what/Wgallery.html*

15. Shibuya and Hachiko

The following three sites have some information (but not a lot) about Shibuya and/or Hachiko. The sites actually are portions of one site (as you may be able to tell by the URL), and you may want to browse through the other offerings. However, to make access easier, each is listed separately below:

> URL: *http://shrine.cyber.ad.jp/~repka/iwshibuya.html*
> (For information and picture of Shibuya.)

> URL: *http://shrine.cyber.ad.jp/~repka/iwhachiko.html*
> (For information about Hachiko the dog.)

> URL: *http://shrine.cyber.ad.jp/~repka/iw_index.html*
> (This is the Tokyo Infoweb. From here you can access the above two sites as well as other information about topics such as chopsticks, Yamanote, yen, etc.)

16. Virtual Traveller

URL: *http://shrine.cyber.ad.jp/~repka/noframes.html*
• Take a Virtual Trip to Tokyo. Start at the airport and be guided along on your journey (with photos and commentary) or choose individual places to visit that interest you (e.g., have noodles for lunch, visit Tokyo Tower, trade travel stories at the Rotenburo—though some of the stories may not be suitable for younger children.)
• Take a Virtual Trip to Mount Fuji. Pay a visit and recount your journey as though you've really been there.
• Traveller's Cafe: This is a chance to ask questions and maybe have them answered (by e-mail).
• Trivia: Random facts about Tokyo and Japan
• Penpals: Requests are mostly from adults (though there are a few teens and younger children listed as well).
• News links: Check out the latest news from Japan
   • Magazines
   • Newspapers (*JamJam*: the Mainichi newspaper, offers entry into an annual haiku-writing competition; "Japan Deep-Down": interviews about different topics related to Japan; other information (an excellent site worth checking out).
     URL: *http://www.mainichi.co.jp/index-e.html*
   • Television (Some are more worth checking out than others.)
• Other links (warning: at least one link is R-rated, adults only. Supervision of students will be necessary, but there is still much good here.)
   • News links

- Regional interest
- Japanese culture (literature, art, history, architecture, religion, sports, food, music)
- Science and technology

Teacher's Notes

Three Events That Helped the World to Focus Its Attention on the Akita:
A) The heart-warming story of the faithful Akita, Hachiko;
B) Helen Keller's involvement with the Akita breed; and
C) The declaration of the Akita as one of Japan's national monuments.
Note: Hachiko has been stuffed and preserved and is displayed at the Japanese Museum of Natural Science in Tokyo.

A Recipe for Modelmaking Sawdust Dough Medium
Ingredients:

8 cups of all-purpose flour
9 cups of fine sawdust through sifting (obtainable at lumberyards for free)
7 cups of boiling water
3 tablespoons of salt

Method:
1. Mix dry ingredients well in a mixing bowl.
2. Add boiling water to the dry mixture.
3. Stir well with a wooden spoon until mixture has consistency of bread dough.
4. When mixture becomes lukewarm, knead well with hand.
5. Use as soon as possible. May be kept for a week in the refrigerator.
6. Cautionary suggestion: Due to the use of boiling water, it is safer for the medium to be made by the teacher or another adult (at home or at school) the day before use.

Bibliography

Ashby, Gwynneth, *Take a Trip to Japan*, Franklin Watts (New York), 1980. Some topics covered are trains, children, food, bathing, rice, and puppet shows. Grade 1+.

Chadwick, Douglas H., "Dead or Alive: The Endangered Species Act," *National Geographic*, March 1995. Five hundred species and subspecies have become extinct in the United States since 1500. The ESA is reshaping the way America society lives on the land. This article looks at the act, its consequences, and its future. Includes a fold-out illustrating all 632 species and subspecies classified as endangered in the 50 states.

Downer, Lesley, *Countries of the World: Japan*, Wayland (Hove, England), 1989. Includes a glossary and information about the bullet train, industry, farming and fishing, a Japanese Elvis look-alike, food, schools, growing up, wildlife, and simple Japanese characters for your students to learn. Grade 3+.

Galvin, Irene Flum, *Exploring Cultures of the World: Japan, a Modern Land with Ancient Roots*, Benchmark Books (New York), 1996. Contains geography and history, the people, family life, festivals and food, school and recreation, the arts, and a glossary at the end. Learn the rules for eating with chopsticks. Did you know that the trains are so crowded during rush-hour in Tokyo that white-gloved men are hired to push people into the trains? Grade 4+.

Glover, Harry, *A Totem Guide: Dogs*. Totem Books (Don Mills, Canada), 1982 An identification guide for early and middle grades.

Graves, William, "Tokyo: A Profile of Success," *National Geographic*, November 1986. Earthquakes and technology are two realities that help define this wealthy, crowded, competitive city. A simple map of the city shows the location of the Shibuya station, home of the Dog Wall.

Haskinss, Jim, *Count Your Way Through Japan*, Carolrhoda Books (Minneapolis), 1987. There is only 1 Fujiyama, you use 2 chopsticks, and there are 3 things to fear in nature.... Keep counting to 10 and learn more about Japan. Grade 1+.

Jacobsen, Karen, *A New True Book: Japan*, Childrens Press (Chicago), 1982. Easy-to-read large text with pictures on every page. Grade 1+.

"Japan," *The Young Children's Encyclopedia, Volume 8*. Encyclopaedia Britannica Inc. (Chicago), 1977. Yukiko and Kozo live in Japan. Kozo, in a village, lives in the old ways, but Yukiko lives in Tokyo, a city that is as modern as any in America. Yukio enjoys many of the old ways especially the holidays. Included is a map and more detail about the country.

Kalman, Bobbie, *Japan: The Culture*, Crabtree Publishing (New York), 1989. Make a paper kimono, an artificial cherry blossom tree, or a samurai helmet after reading about such things. Grade 2+.

Kalman, Bobbie, *Japan: The Land*, Crabtree Publishing (New York), 1989. Children can test their samurai-Q, learn about earthquakes, winds and giant waves, and match pictures with descriptions of life in Japan. Grade 2+.

Linderman, Joan M. and Virginia Funk, *The New Complete Akita*, Howell Brook House (New York), 1994. The history of the breed, the care of Akitas, and plenty of photographs. A teacher resource.

Posell, Elsa, "The True Book of Dogs," *I Want to Know About...,Volume 10*. Childrens Press (Chicago), 1972. Dogs are man's best friend. Beginning readers can learn about types of dogs and what they are best at, plus how to care for their own dogs.

"Railroad Systems," *Growing up with Science: The Illustrated Encyclopedia of Invention, Volume 13*. H.S. Stuttman (Westport, Connecticut), 1984. This article looks at various kinds of signalling devices, traffic control, and computerization. (Use as a resource for the science activity on trains.)

Smith, Patrick, "Inner Japan," *National Geographic*, September 1994. Away from Tokyo, towards the western coastline, one finds the tranquility, traditions, and closeness-to-nature of the back of Japan.

"Tokyo," *Disney's Wonderful World of Knowledge, Volume 17: Great Capitals*. Danbury Press (Danbury, Connecticut), 1973. Grandma Duck and Goofy take the reader on a tour of Tokyo; includes history and photos.

"Underground Railway Systems," *Growing up with Science: The Illustrated Encyclopedia of Invention, Volume 20*. H.S. Stuttman (Westport, Connecticut), 1984. For underground trains, tunnels are needed and there are different kinds. The London, England Victoria Lines uses electronic codes to drive the train. A full-page drawing shows how these signals work. Other topics covered are the trains themselves and safety. A useful article for the science activity on trains.

Wells, Ruth and Yoshi, *A to Zen*, Picture Book Studio (Saxonville, Massachusetts), 1992. In true Japanese fashion, this book begins at the "back" cover. "A" for Aikido, "F" for futon, "J" for Janken, "O" for origami, "R" for Randoseru, and "U" for Ukiyo-e. What do all these words mean? Grade 1+.

"What Kind of Dog is That?" *The Young Children's Encyclopedia, Volume 4*. Encyclopaedia Britannica Inc. (Chicago), 1977. Andy wants to enter his dog into the dog show, but he needs to know what kind of dog he has. As different children pass by, he asks them what kind of dog they have. Finally his teacher walks by with her poodle and helps Andy get into the show. Dogs of various breeds are shown and named.

"Where Am I?," *The Young Children's Encyclopedia, Volume 13*. Encyclopaedia Britannica Inc. (Chicago), 1977. A description of Tokyo for the children to guess.

Wall 10   Dikes in the Netherlands: A National Character

Pre-Reading Warm-Up

1. The Building of a People

Throughout history, even until the present time, the Dutch have shown the world that they are a people characterized as resourceful, determined, and persistent in their unrelenting struggle with the sea. This human spirit is most aptly captured in a fictional story, *The Hole in the Dike*, created by an American, Mary Mapes Dodge, in 1906. She retold the story in her famous *Hans Brinker or The Silver Skates*, and the story has been told again by more recent authors. Lenny Hart's *The Boy Who Held Back the Sea* features beautiful paintings of the Dutch landscape by Thomas Locker, and Norma Green's *The Hole in the Dike* is yet another retelling of this story. Obtain a copy of one of these books and read it to your class.

Although the famous story of a brave Dutch boy, Peter (or Pieter, in Dutch), is a work of fiction, it soon became known worldwide. The story describes the character of the Dutch people so well that a statue of Peter, the fictional Dutch hero, was erected by the municipality of Haarlem (the town where the legendary heroics were supposed to have happened) at Spaarndam, the outskirts of town. The statue was unveiled by Princess Margriet in 1950.

A) Ask your students if there are any other monuments erected and/or commemorative events celebrated around fictional stories and characters. Examples are the statue and re-enactment of the Pied Piper of Hamlin in Germany and the statue of Peter Pan in Kensington Garden in London.

B) Repeat the same activity with real stories. An example is the Winnie the Bear statue in Winnipeg, Manitoba, Canada. (The *Winnie the Pooh* stories were based on a real bear cub found in the northern Ontario wilds by a soldier on his way to war. He named the bear Winnie after his home town Winnipeg and left him in the London zoo for safe keeping. A. A. Milne and his son loved visiting Winnie at the zoo and thus the stories were created.)

Language Arts

2. Story Reading

Read stories to your young students about the Dutch and/or provide them with a collection of stories and books about the Dutch which they can read themselves (see the bibliography at the end of this chapter for some suggestions).

3. Letter Writing

If Internet resources are not available to your students, writing letters to seek information is certainly a most worthwhile exercise. The following addresses are provided for your use.

In the USA	In Canada
Embassy of the Kingdom of the Netherlands	Embassy of the Kingdom of the Netherlands
4200 Linnean Avenue, NW	350 Albert Street, Suite 2020
Washington, DC 20008	Ottawa, Ontario
USA	Canada
Ph. (202) 244-5300; Fax (202) 362-3430	K1R 1A4
	Ph. (613) 237-5030; Fax (613) 237-6471

In the Netherlands
Bonaire Government Tourist Board
Kaya Simon Bolivar 12
Kralendijk, Bonaire
Holland
Ph. (7) 8322; Fax (7) 8408

4. Fiction Writing: "Before the Drowning Begins"

In the Netherlands, archaeologists have discovered ruins of an ancient village and a fortress (the long lost Zeeland village of Valkenisse and the fortress Keizershoofd) below sea level at ebb tide. They disappeared in 1682 in the North Sea. Like the destruction of Pompei and the legendary Atlantis by Nature, early Dutch inhabitants were caught unaware by the encroaching sea and perished.

Ask your students to pretend that they are villagers of historic Valkenisse. Assign them to write a short story recounting how their daily lives are being affected by the ominous apprehension of living next to the devouring North Sea. In like manner, they can write about their anxiety if they live near the fault line on the West Coast of North America.

5. A Study of Anne Frank: A Dutch Holocaust Connection

Behind a bookcase in one of the rooms at 263 Prinsengracht in Amsterdam was the famous hiding place where the Jewish girl, Anne Frank, and her family lived in the midst of Nazi persecution during the Second World War. The hiding place, whose walls still display the magazine and newspaper clippings and pictures stuck there by the Frank family, is now preserved as a national museum. The Anne Frank House has now been turned into an international youth center for the promotion of understanding in the spirit of the diary. Anne Frank's own words found in her famous diary testify to the good side of human nature:

"In spite of everything, I still believe that people are really good at heart. If I look up into the heavens, I think that it will all come right, that this cruelty too will end, and that peace and tranquility will return again."

Embark on a class study of the story of Anne Frank by using a range of materials, including the primary source, *The Diary of Anne Frank*, biographies of Anne Frank, and Internet sites on Anne Frank. One such site introduces us to the Anne Frank House in Amsterdam.
URL is: *http://www.channels.nl/annefran.html*

To contact the Anne Frank House in Holland, please use the following:
The Anne Frank House
Prinsengracht 263
Amsterdam
Holland
Ph. +31 (0) 20-5567100
Fax +31 (0) 20-6207999

When the heart-wrenching story of Anne Frank is fully appreciated for all its implications, lead your class to undertake studying the lives of other famous people who have taught the world positive lessons by which to live with courage and honesty and in peace and harmony. Some examples are Ghandi, Martin Luther King, Jr., Mother Teresa, and Nelson Mandela.

You may wish to link this activity with the chapter on the Holocaust earlier in this book.

6. Editorial Writing and Debate: "To Dike or Not To Dike?"

Nature is a formidable and tenacious force. In most cases throughout human history, Nature has demonstrated the winning hand in its battle with man. There was a great deal of controversy about dike-building during the floods in the U.S. Midwest in the summer of 1993. Dikes are said to have created problems because the rivers had been prevented from taking their natural courses as they swelled and spilled over in low-lying areas. On the other hand, without dikes, the Netherlands and part of Belgium would be substantially reduced in size.

Assign your students to research and write opposing views, in the form of journalistic editorials, of the usefulness and effectiveness of dikes. Using the written material, organize formal debates on the motion that "Dikes Illustrate That Man Conquers Nature."

Social Studies

7. What's In A Name?

This coastal country in Continental Europe has two names: the Netherlands (or Nederlands, as known locally) meaning "low lands," and Holland, meaning "hollow or marshy land." The inhabitants are called Dutch, a corruption of the German's Detach, perhaps inferring that many Hollanders and Germans come from low lands.

Help your class to identify places whose names sum up succinctly the characteristics of those places, such as Iceland and Long Beach. Does your town's name have a special meaning? Ask your students about it.

8. Migration History

Throughout history, as people migrate from one place to another, there is a tendency to build up the new community to resemble the immigrants' homeland. In fact, the new settlement might be named after the place from where they came. New York is one such example. Early Dutch explorers founded New Amsterdam when they first set foot in North America. New Amsterdam later became New York.

Ask students to think of places around the world whose names were given as a commemoration of other places. Examples are: New England, New Orleans, New Mexico, and Nova Scotia.

9. A Social Studies Fair on the Dutch Society and Culture

Ask your students what they know about Holland and list their information on the chalkboard. Then ask them what they'd like to know. The teacher can add suggestions. Assign each working group of three students the some topics for research. Each group will then present its findings succinctly on a presentation poster board, the kind used in most school science fairs. (Please refer to "Teacher's Notes" for more information on how to construct presentation poster boards.)
Topics of research on Dutch society and culture could be:
* Dikes
* Windmills
* Wooden shoes
* Flowers and tulips
* Art and artists
* Traditional clothings
* Folk tales and legends
* Anne Frank
* Dairy products and candies
* Canals and bridges

10. Contour Map Study

This unit of learning consists of four hands-on activities which are designed to be performed sequentially and incrementally from the first activity to the fourth one. Each activity is meant for a single lesson or several lessons.

A) First Activity: A Simple Above-Sea-Level Topography

Duplicate a simple contour map as shown on the right (Diagram 1).
Teach your class what sea level means. With that point of reference, help your students understand the increments of rise in the landform according to the contour lines (e.g. 50 feet, 100 feet, 150 feet etc.) Ask the students to visualize what that land form looks like.

On the chalkboard, with the use of a yard (meter) stick, draw a graph. Show your class how the topographical information (in the form of contour lines) can be transposed into a cross-sectional diagram of the land form shown on the map (Diagram 2).

Instruct your students to try the same cross-section diagram on graph paper.

B) Second Activity: Above- and Below-Sea-Level Topographies

Use sea level (as indicated by zero on a contour map) to introduce to your class the concept of underwater topography. Provide your class with another simple home-spun contour map which shows underwater contour lines (Diagram 3). Ask your students to shade the underwater terrain with shades of blue, dark blue for the deeper gradients, and lighter shades of blue for the shallower gradients. Instruct them to use green for land at sea level, and shades of brown for ascending land, with darker shades for the higher grounds.

On graph paper, once again ask students to transpose the topographical data into a cross-section diagram of the map, showing underwater land masses (Diagram 4).

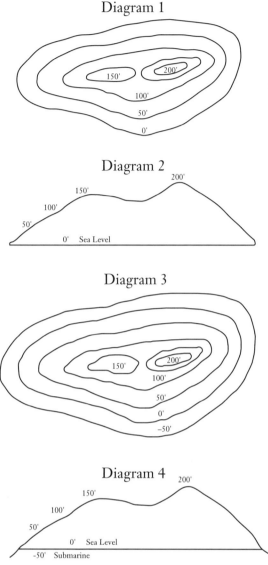

Diagram 1

Diagram 2

Diagram 3

Diagram 4

C) Third Activity: Understanding the Topography of Your Town / City

From your local public library or government land office, obtain a contour map of your town/city. Explore with your class the contours of the land around your community. As a small group exercise, ask students to identify the low-lying areas in your city and color them blue. Ask them to check out from various sources (such as local emergency response organizations, their parents, etc.) if the low-lying areas they have identified are indeed the areas most susceptible to flooding.

If those areas do not suffer from flooding, ask your students to find out why not. Have counter-flooding measures been put in place?

D) Fourth Activity: Understanding the Topography of the Netherlands

In the Netherlands, more than half of the population lives on land that could easily be flooded at high tide if no dikes had been erected to prevent this from happening.

Provide groups of three students with contour maps of the Netherlands and adjacent Belgium. Ask them to identify the land that is below sea level and to color it blue. Provide an opportunity for each group to present and explain their findings. Ask them to guess the extent of land loss if the dike system was not in place in the Netherlands.

Science

11. Windmills

Windmills are one thing that comes to mind when we think of Holland. They were used to pump water from low-lying areas and reclaim land for farming. In other places, windmills have been used to crush grain into flour and extract oil from seeds and juice from sugar cane. Show your class pictures of various styles of windmills. Modern-day ones look very different from the ones of a hundred years or more ago. If your students are young, draw a simple cut-away diagram of a windmill and show them how to label the key components (sails, fantail, building, post, millstone, gears). Older students can draw their own windmills and label them (see the bibliography at the end of this chapter for resources).

12. A Class Discussion on How Man Influences the Natural Order

Our natural environment around the globe, over the last thousand years, has changed due to human influences. Facilitate a discussion on the effects each step of human "progress" has had on our ecosystem.

13. Building Dikes before Modern Technology

Pose this question to your students: "How would dikes have been built before there were heavy equipment and modern-day architectural and engineering technologies?" (Please refer to the "Teacher's Notes" for information on the Delta Projects, the greatest engineering project the Dutch have ever tackled.) Assist your students in accessing information that helps answer the above question. (One such resource is "Land Reclamation" listed in the bibliography at the end of this chapter.)

14. Flood Control

Two methods of controlling flooding are used in the United States: 1) Control the water levels and 2) Keep floodwaters within a certain area. Study with your students how this is done, and which is most effective. Which method is used in your community? Why? "Flood Control" (see the bibliography at the end of this chapter) contains diagrams and drawings to illustrate some of the methods used to control flooding.

Mathematics

15. Measurement: Area

Trace the outline of a map of Holland onto graph paper and shade in that area of the country that is below sea level (a good atlas, such as *Britannica Atlas*, will show this area in a different color). Ask the students to calculate what fraction or decimal of land is below sea level (approximately one fourth). If you assign scale to the graph paper (e.g., 1 square on the graph equals 50 square miles or kilometers), the students can also estimate the area by counting the squares or portions thereof. (See also Activity #10.)

Arts and Crafts

16. Drawing

Read or tell the students the story of the hole in the dike. Provide them with large sheets of drawing paper and ask them to draw a scene from the story and retell it. Perhaps they can try to include as many other aspects of traditional Dutch culture in their pictures as possible: tulips, wooden shoes, windmills, etc.

Food Experience

17. Recipes

Uitsmijters
(This is one of Holland's favorite lunch dishes.)

Ingredients:
>6 slices white bread
>6 eggs
>12 slices ham or roast beef
>Butter
>Salt, pepper and mustard
>Pickles

Method:
1. Butter each slice of bread.
2. Add 2 slices of meat to each, completely covering the bread.
3. Fry the eggs soft and add one to each slice of bread.
4. Serve with seasonings and pickles.

Internet Resources

18. Frequently Asked Questions (FAQ) about Holland

Does your class have questions about Holland? Here is a great place to get the answers. Sections 4, 5, and 6 will probably be the most useful for your class. To access, you can go to:
URL: *http://www.sci.kun.nl/scn_faq/index.html*

- History/Culture: In this section you will find answers to questions about korfball, Sinterklaas, literature, population, Queen's Day, Hans Brinker, etc.
- Recipes: What do the Dutch like to eat? How do you prepare it? If the one recipe included in this chapter is not to your liking, try checking out these others.
- The Rest: This is a miscellaneous section which covers topics such as "flappentap," expressions using the word "Dutch," the Internet in the Netherlands, banks, phones, etc.

19. Facts and Map of Holland

URL: *http://www.ic.gov/94fact/country/17l.html*
or
URL: *http://www.odci.gov/cia/publications/95fact/nl.html*

20. Koninklijke Bibliotheek

This museum in Holland has graciously made available, on the Internet, 100 highlights of its collection of old manuscripts, engravings, lithographs, woodcuts, drawings, etc. A photo (enlargeable to full screen size) and ample commentary can be found for each item. The titles are all in Dutch, but don't be fooled. The photos are incredible and the descriptions are in English. Check it out at:
URL: *http://www.konbib.nl/100hoogte/menu-tours-en.html#hss*

21. Environmental History of Holland

"The Dutch clearly have significant cause to be concerned about global warming, especially possible rising sea levels." This site takes a quick look at the history of the land and addresses some of the environmental problems that are unique to the Netherlands. Although these articles are more suited to high school students, a teacher of younger students could summarize the material and guide students in a discussion about the environmental concerns that affect not only Holland but their own community as well.

URL: *http://www.rri.org/envatlas/europe/netherlands/nl-hist.html*
and
URL: *http://www.rri.org/envatlas/europe/netherlands/nl-conc.html*

Teacher's Notes

Making Presentation Poster Boards:

The average dimensions of a presentation poster board are 3 feet (1 meter) tall by 6 feet (2 meters) wide. Obtain refrigerator/freezer/stove cardboard boxes from your local major appliances store. With a sharp carpet or utility knife, cut out 3' x 6' (1m x2m) pieces. Fold both ends of the 6 feet (2m) length at 1.5 feet (0.5m) each. Now, you have constructed a self-supporting folding poster board. Students may cover the cardboard with attractive art paper of different colors. Pictures, written information, graphs, etc., may be glued on the poster board, ready for presentation and display.

The Delta Projects:

In the province of Zeeland, south of Rotterdam, the Delta Projects, the greatest engineering feat the Dutch people have ever undertaken, has been under construction for the past thirty-four years. The last stage of the project, the construction of a movable marine flood gate across the estuary of the Oosterschelde River, is almost in place. The structure is designed to protect southwest Holland from any disasters like the flood of 1953, when a fierce storm combined with spring flooding caused havoc in that area, flooding Rotterdam and the Cathedral of Dordrecht.

Bibliography

See also the bibliography at the end of the chapter on the Holocaust for more books about Anne Frank.

Dodge, Mary Mapes, *Hans Brinker or The Silver Skates*. Charles Scribner's Sons (New York), 1915. It is this novel that has really fostered the story of Peter and the hole in the dike. Hans and Gretel want to enter the iceskating race, but their mother is too poor to buy skates for them. Dodge weaves a fine picture of life in Holland in this children's classic.

"Earth the Home of Man," *Disney's Wonderful World of Knowledge, Volume 2: Nature*. Danbury Press (Danbury, Connecticut), 1973. Donald Duck leads the students in understanding the importance of respecting our environment. (Useful for Activities #12 and 21).

"Ecology," *Growing up with Science: The Illustrated Encyclopedia of Invention, Volume 5*. H.S. Stuttman, (Westport, Connecticut), 1984. In order to understand how man has affected the ecosystem (Activities #12 and #21) the ecosystem must be understood. This four-page, illustrated article is useful for that purpose.

Everett Fisher, Leonard, *Kinderdike*, Macmillan (New York), 1994. Based on a legend about a town in the Netherlands that rebuilt after a horrible flood. A great read-aloud for younger children.

Fairclough, Chris, *Take a Trip to Holland*, Franklin Watts (New York), 1982. With large, easy-to-read print, Fairclough makes a tour of Holland accessible to even the youngest students.

"Flood Control," *Growing up with Science: The Illustrated Encyclopedia of Invention, Volume 6*. H.S. Stuttman, (Westport, Connecticut), 1984. River flooding, reservoirs, miscellaneous methods, tidal flooding, the Thames barrier, chain of reservoirs, overflow channels, and river barriers are all covered in this article with excellent diagrams and illustrations.

Green, Norma, *The Hole in the Dike*. Thomas Y. Crowell (New York), 1974. A picture book which the author acknowledges is adapted from *Hans Brinker or The Silver Skates* by M.M. Dodge.

Hart, Lenny, *The Boy Who Held Back the Sea*. Dial Press (New York), 1987. Features beautiful Dutch landscape paintings by Thomas Locker.

Huggett, Frank, *Netherlands: The Land and Its People*, MacDonald Educational (London), 1980. Illustrated with a mix of photographs and humorous drawings. Students can observe the process of making wooden shoes, see a typical day's menu, and even try some recipes. Grade 3+.

James, Ian, *Inside the Netherlands*, Franklin Watts (New York), 1990. Shows a map, a pictorial population density comparison with four countries, the Delta plan, industry, the arts, sports, food, and the land. Grade 3+.

"Land Reclamation," *Growing up with Science: The Illustrated Encyclopedia of Invention, Volume 8.* H.S. Stuttman, (Westport, Connecticut), 1984. Discusses the techniques used in reclaiming land in the Netherlands as well as in swamps, deserts, and marginal land.

"Life in a Greenhouse," *Disney's Wonderful World of Knowledge Yearbook 1990*. Grolier Enterprises (Danbury, Connecticut), 1990. The greenhouse effect concerns the Dutch. This looks at why scientists think the world is heating up and how. Also included is what we can do to stop or slow down the warming.

"Our Fragile Earth: It's the Only Home We Have." *Disney's Wonderful World of Knowledge Yearbook 1991*. Grolier Enterprises (Danbury, Connecticut) 1991. Threatened wildlife, pollution, the ozone layer, global warming and toxic wastes are all environmental concerns.

Seward, Pat, *Cultures of the World: Netherlands*, Marshall Cavendish (New York), 1995. A simple map shows land below sea level and reclaimed land. Learn more about dikes, the Delta Project, reclaiming the land, plus all your Grade 4 students ever wanted to know about Holland.

Spier, Peter, *Of Dikes and Windmills*, Doubleday (Garden City, New York), 1969. If you only provide one book for your classroom on this topic, this is the one, despite its age. It is too good to miss. Spier tells the story of Holland and her war against the sea in a very engaging manner, with delightful and informative illustrations. Grade 5+ can read this themselves, but a creative teacher can adapt its use to younger students.

"Windmill", *Growing up with Science: The Illustrated Encyclopedia of Invention, Volume 23*, H.S. Stuttman (Westport, Connecticut), 1984. The windmill was first invented in Persia, about 1,400 years ago, and didn't arrive in Europe until 1150 with a different design. The article looks at the beginnings of windmills and includes a cutaway drawing of an 18th-century windmill.

"Windmill in Trouble," *The Young Children's Encyclopedia, Volume 16*. Encyclopaedia Britannica, Inc. (Chicago), 1977. Piet lives in a windmill in Holland. He loves to watch the arms as they pump the water off the land. One day he is left alone in the windmill; a big wind comes up, and he must get those huge arms to stop or the windmill might be swept away.

"Windmill and Wind Pump," *Growing up with Science: The Illustrated Encyclopedia of Invention, Volume 22*. H.S. Stuttman (Westport, Connecticut), 1984. Various kinds of windmills are pictured and discussed in this article. A detailed, labeled diagram of the windmill parts and operation will assist students in the science activity on windmills.

Wall 11   Northern Ireland: Peace Line in a War Zone

Pre-Reading Warm-Up

1. Irish Folk Music: The Orange and the Green

The Troubles in Ireland have been the subject of many folk ballads. Obtain some Irish folk albums, tapes, or compact discs from your public library. Select some songs that narrate the Irish anguish over the years. Duplicate the song lyrics for your class to follow as you play the songs in class. Discuss the emotions expressed in those songs. Some Irish folk songs that are relevant to the struggles in Ireland over the years are suggested below:

- "The Orange and the Green" by the Irish Rovers (Please see "Teacher's Notes" for song lyrics of "The Orange and the Green")
- "The Wind that Shakes the Corn" by the Irish Rovers
- "Rocky Road to Dublin" by the Clancy Brothers and Tommy Makem
- "The West's Awake" by the Clancy Brothers and Tommy Makem
- "Green in Green" by The Clancy Brothers and Tommy Makem
- Mrs. McGrath" by Pete Seeger

Language Arts

2. Story Time

Read some Irish folklore to your students or provide books and stories for them to read (see the bibliography at the end of this chapter).

3. Pen Pals for Students

The British Information Services provide the following contact addresses for school children around the world to establish contact with the children and adults of Northern Ireland. Encourage your students to become ongoing pen pals with Northern Irish students of their own age.

For pen pals throughout the United Kingdom, classroom requests from teachers must include the name, gender, age, address and special interests of each member of the class. The address is as follows:

Links Section,
Central Bureau for Educational Visits and Exchanges,
16 Malone Road
Belfast BT9 5BN
Northern Ireland

Friends by Post, a voluntary organization, seeks to help people of similar ages and interests to establish a regular exchange of news and views. The address is as follows:

Friends by Post,
43 Chatsworth Road, High Lane,
Stockpot,
Cheshire SK6 8DA
England

The Pen Friend League International, established in 1968, encourages greater understanding between different peoples of the world through establishing lasting pen friendships. Pen friends can be arranged from anywhere around the world and there is no age limit. The League operates a school section which can assist North American schools and colleges in finding pen friends in the British Isles. The address is as follows:

Pen Friend League International
143 Oscott School Lane,
Great Bar,
Birmingham B44 9EL
England

The Royal Mail International Pen Pal Club is open to all North American residents, between the age of nine and eighteen, who would like to write to a British pen pal. Parent/guardian-signed permission is required.

4. Creative Writing: War and Peace Through the Eye of a Child

Northern Ireland is a land in delicate balance. A powerful explosion in London's docklands area on February 9, 1996, believed to have been set off by the Irish Republican Army, shattered the dream of peace and a 17-month IRA cease-fire that began on August 31, 1994.

After you've had a chance to share some of Ireland's history with your students. ask them to write on one of the following:

A) You are a child/youth living in Belfast, Northern Ireland. This is December of 1994. Write in your diary about your feelings of enjoying peace at last this holiday season. Describe the changes of mood in your family, neighborhood, and city. Talk about the things you and your family are doing to celebrate a peaceful holiday in Northern Ireland.

B) You are a child/youth living in Belfast, Northern Ireland. Today is February 10, 1996. Less than 24 hours ago, a powerful explosion occurred in the dockside area of London only hours after the IRA had made a public statement that they were ending the peace talks with the British government. Enter in your diary your feelings of a shattered dream, fear, and a sense of powerlessness and hopelessness. Describe the mood in your family, community, and city. What are you and your family doing to cope with this loss of precious and fragile peace?

Social Studies

5. St. Patrick's Day: Celebrating the Irish Culture

Irish culture is a wealth of folklore, myths, and religion. The unicorn, the leprechauns, the shamrock, and the legend of St. Patrick casting snakes and vipers out of Ireland are but some of the many fascinating culture traits that have enriched Irish literature, music, art, and thought.

Invite a member of the local Irish Cultural Center to speak to your class with a display of cultural artifacts. On or around St. Patrick's Day, March 17, organize an Irish celebration complete with Irish music, bulletin boards of displays, and Irish food.

6. Social Participation Towards Peace in Northern Ireland

Follow the peace talks throughout the year, and a week or two before St. Patrick's Day (March 17), organize a student-letter writing campaign, urging for the return of peace to Northern Ireland and England with the continuation of peace talks between the disputants in the conflict.

Collect students' letters, poems, artwork, banners, posters, and other messages of peace. Send them to both Prime Minister John Major and to Sinn Fein President Gerry Adams at the following addresses:

Mr. Gerry Adams, President,
Sinn Fein Head Office,
44 Parnell Square,
Dublin 1,
Ireland
Ph. (+353-1) 8726100 or (+353-1) 8726839
Fax (+353-1) 8733074

Sinn Fein Foreign Affairs Bureau,
51/55 Falls Road,
Belfast, Northern Ireland
Ph. (+44-1232) 624421;Fax (+44-1232) 622112

Irish Northern Aid Committee,
363 Seventh Avenue,
New York, NY 10001,
USA
Ph. (212) 736-1916
Fax (212) 279-1916

The Rt. Hon. Mr. John Major, M.P.,
Prime Minister of the United Kingdom,
10 Downing Street,
London SWIA 2AA,
England
Ph. (0171) 270-3000

In the USA

Embassy of the U.K. of Great Britain and
    Northern Ireland
3100 Massachusetts Avenue, NW,
Washington, D.C. 20008,
USA
Ph. (202) 462-1340; Fax (202) 898-4255

In Canada

The High Commissioner of the U.K. of
    Great Britain and Northern Ireland
80 Elgin Street,
Ottawa, Ontario
Canada, K1P 5K7
Ph. (613) 237-1530; Fax (613) 237-7980

7. The Natural Beauty of Ireland: Be An Armchair Tourist

Despite the ugliness created by war in Northern Ireland, the six counties are a beautiful land of blue mountains and forest parks, mazy lakes and windswept moors, white Atlantic sands, and an inland sea. Dozens of small towns and villages are hidden away among the greenery of the countryside, and fishing villages are strung out along the shores. The towers and steeples of parish churches and castle ruins mark the high ground beyond trimmed hedgerows. The city of Belfast, as an example, is described by one writer as a "Hibernian Rio," ringed by high hills, sea lough, and river valley.

To approach the study of Northern Ireland from a picturesque angle, borrow from your school district library or the public library scenic films or videos of Ireland. At the same time, encourage your students to write to the following Northern Ireland Tourist Board offices for tourist information which certainly contains descriptions and pictures of beautiful Northern Ireland.

U.S. Office

Northern Ireland Tourist Board
551 Fifth Avenue, Suite 701
New York, NY 10176
USA
Ph. (212) 922-0101 or 1-800-326-0036
Fax (212) 922-0099

Canadian Office

Northern Ireland Tourist Board
111 Avenue Road, Suite 450
Toronto, Ontario
Canada, M5R 3J8
Ph. (416) 925-6368; Fax (416) 961-2175

In Northern Ireland

Northern Ireland Tourist Board
St. Anne's Court,
59 North Street,
Belfast BT1 1NB
Northern Ireland
Ph. (011232) 246609; Fax (011232) 240960

8. Peace Line in a War Zone in Northern Ireland: A Discussion

In the city of Belfast, in Northern Ireland, "the Troubles" had their most pronounced effect in the working class neighborhoods of the Protestant Shankill and Catholic Falls Road communities where most of the bombings, shootings, and murders have occurred. These two communities of the same people are separated by a thirty-foot wall, crowned with barbed wire, euphemistically and ironically called the "Peace Line," that runs down the middle of the lanes they share.

Discuss with your class how peace may be achieved, be it at home with siblings and parents, at school with schoolmates and teachers, in our country with fellow citizens, and in the world with other planet dwellers.

Can peace be achieved through threats of physical violence? Can a "Peace Line" or barricade bring about peace? What do we truly need to bring about peace? Discuss.

9. A Unit of Study on the British Isles

Plan a unit of lessons in learning the geography of the British Isles and a history of their people.

Lesson 1

Either provide students with an outline map of the British Isles or ask them to trace the map outline over a map of Britain. Instruct them to label the political boundaries of the different political and cultural entities of this country also known as the United Kingdom. Ask them to describe those entities. Students will be interested to find out that the Union Jack, the national flag of the United Kingdom, is a combination of national symbols of Ireland, Wales, Scotland, and England.

Using color pencils, students will color the different political entities of Britain. Ask them to color Northern Ireland with a different color than the rest of Ireland, the Republic of Ireland, which is also known as Eire. They should identify the capital cities of these places and label their locations on their own maps.

Lesson 2

Teach an encapsulated and simplified version of the history of Britain. With the assistance of your teacher-librarian, locate abridged or simplified versions of British history through interlibrary loans. Organize your class into working groups (not more than three students per group), and assign research projects on the history of Britain. Pose the critical question: In what ways are the English and Irish peoples different?

Lesson 3

Help your students obtain books about contemporary Northern Ireland.

Rotate members of the triad work groups, and ask them to respond to the following germinal questions:

A) What was the cause of the problem (known as "the Troubles") in Ireland?

B) What historic events led up to the partitioning of Ireland?

C) How have the Irish people been coping with the long-standing trouble in Northern Ireland?

D) What attempts have been made, and by whom, to bring peace to Northern Ireland?

E) What are the latest developments in the peace process? (Provide students with an account of the latest news about Northern Ireland from the media.)

10. Church History: The Catholics and the Protestants

For centuries, the Roman Catholic Church was the only dominant Christian Church/denomination which held great spiritual and temporal powers over the lives of kings and queens and common people until two events that occurred independently. One was Martin Luther nailing 95 theses on the door of All Saints Church in Wittenburg, Germany, on the eve of All Saints Day, 1517, denouncing the

Roman Catholic Church's belief in salvation by works, which led to his excommunication from the church and the beginning of the Protestant Reformation throughout Europe.

The other event was King Henry VIII's separation from the Catholic Church in 1534. The Catholic pope in Rome refused to nullify King Henry's marriage to Queen Catherine of Aragon (divorce was forbidden by the church and all authority came from the Pope, even to kings themselves), so Henry VIII passed a new law in England called the Act of Supremacy, which made him head of the church in England instead of the pope. This allowed him to give himself a divorce and marry Anne Boleyn. The new church was called the Church of England, and is also known as the Anglican Church or, in the U.S., Episcopalian. Throughout the next two centuries, many Christian groups broke away from the Roman Catholic Church and became known as Protestants because they, for different reasons, protested against some of the beliefs and/or practices of the Roman Catholic Church and the papacy itself.

The sectarian conflict in Northern Ireland, by and large, was fueled by denominational difference as well as ideological reason. The dichotomy between the republicans and the unionists, and the Catholics and the Protestants, has been symbolized by the colors of green and orange, respectively.

Lead your class in learning more about the division in the same people in Northern Ireland.

11. A People Divided: A Study of Human Conflict

The people of Northern Ireland have been engaged in an internal strife for years. Lead your students in examining the internal disagreements and the resultant wars that occurred throughout history. Also, refer to some contemporary examples.

Some examples are the American Civil War, the Struggle between the Nationalists and the Communists in China, the Spanish Civil War, the Partition of Korea into North and South Korea, the struggle for self-determination by the aboriginal peoples of the Americas, and Quebec's determination to separate from the rest of Canada, just to name a few.

Discuss whether the historical conflicts had reaped positive results or not. What lessons can your students draw from the history of human conflict?

12. Diplomacy of Negotiation or the Power of the Gun

On the other side of the world, there is another development which eerily resembles the Troubles in Northern Ireland and has drawn equal global attention: the suicide bombings in Israel by a radical Muslim group, Hamas, since February 25, 1996.

The Jews in South Africa are outraged by the willingness of the South African President, Nelson Mandela, to meet with a group of visiting representatives of Hamas in April, 1996. In a March 7, 1996 Reuter newsstory, Mr. Nelson Mandela is quoted as saying that while he condemns the bombings in Israel, he is willing to meet with Hamas representatives when they arrive: "My attitude is to see everybody who wants to see me, whether I agree with his policy or not."

Discuss with your class whether or not Mr. Mandela's attitude is correct, and whether his intended actions are appropriate in bringing about peace in the Middle East. Does diplomacy of good will and negotiation supersede the power of gunpowder? Discuss.

Science

13. Grow Potatoes

Potatoes are an important part of the Irish economy. Obtain seed potatoes and give one to each student (if space is limited, students could share). Allow them to examine the potatoes and count the eyes. Each eye is a potential bud. Have each student record his/her observations and then label the potatoes with the students' names and put them in a dark place. Once a week the students remove their potatoes from the dark and record the changes they observe. They eyes (buds) should sprout.

Once the sprouts are no longer than one inch (2.5 cm) the potatoes can be planted. If timing and weather permit, plant outside (if your school has space for this). In a sunny location, dig a 9-inch-deep (22-cm) trench, long enough for each potato to be placed 2 feet apart (or dig more than one trench, each trench being 2 feet apart). Spread a 3-inch-thick (7-cm) layer of peat at the bottom of the trench and place the potatoes, sprouts up, in the peat, 2 feet apart. Place more peat around the tubers and then fill the remaining space with soil. Alternatively, one or two potatoes could be grown in the classroom in a large tub by a sunny window. The students should water regularly and continue their weekly journalling.

The potatoes are ready to dig up when the foliage begins to die down. However, they can be dug up earlier for smaller potatoes. How many potatoes did each seed potato produce? What was the average number (per seed potato) produced?

Now, boil or bake the potatoes and serve with salt and butter. Mmmm good!

Mathematics

14. Population

In Northern Ireland, one-third of the population is Roman Catholic. In the Republic of Ireland more than 90% is Roman Catholic. In 1994, the population of the Republic was 3,512,000. How many people were Catholic? Protestant? In 1992 the population of Northern Ireland was 1,610,00. How many were Protestant? Catholic? (Statistics are from *Encyclopaedia Britannica 1995 Book of the Year* and *Encyclopaedia Britannica Macropaedia Volume 13, 15th edition.*)

Arts and Crafts

15. Cultural Symbols

Assign your students to research a cultural symbol of Ireland and to find out if it is a symbol of Northern Ireland, the Republic of Ireland, or both. Provide the students with construction paper and art supplies and help them re-create the symbols. Use the symbols as a bulletin board border.

Food Experience

16. Recipes

Although the potato is not native to Ireland but to South America, by 1845 the Irish had become so dependent upon the potato as the main ingredient in their diet that when a fungus destroyed the potato crop that year, the entire nation starved. A million Irish left their homeland, many coming to North America. Below is an Irish recipe that depends upon the potato.

Potato Candy

Children love candy, but parents and teachers are always concerned with nutrition. Here is a recipe that meets the desires of both!

Ingredients:

     Potatoes, mashed and cooled (one potato per four students)
     Confectioner's sugar (icing sugar)
     Peanut butter (smooth or crunchy it doesn't matter)
     Waxed paper or plastic wrap

     Method:

1. Place potatoes into a bowl and add sugar gradually until a dough is formed (if the potato is warm the sugar will melt and more will be needed). The students will likely need your supervision to know when to stop adding sugar, unless they have a fair bit of kitchen experience.

2. When dough is thick enough to roll, roll it 1/4 inch thick.
3. Spread with peanut butter (If any of your students are allergic to peanuts, keep some of the dough separate from the peanut butter so that they can still sample it.)
4. Roll it up like a jelly roll, beginning at longest side.
5. Wrap in waxed paper or plastic wrap.
6. Refrigerate until somewhat hardened.
7. Slice and share.

Internet Resources

17. The Latest News

For the latest news on the peace process, including pictures, go to:
URL: *http://www.nireland.com/peace/*

18. Hope for Peace: Add Your Voices for Peace Across the Miles

Your class can show its support for peace in Northern Ireland by offering comments in the "Peace Book" at the Peace Web Site (URL above). The e-mail address of the Peace Web Site is *peace@revelations.co.uk*. For excerpts of comments already sent by others see "Teachers Notes."

19. The Peace Process

On August 31, 1994, a cease-fire was agreed upon between the British government and the IRA. An International Body on Arms Decommissioning was set up to launch in Northern Ireland the so-called "twin track" process: peace talks that occur simultaneously with arms decommissioning.

The break-off in peace talks as demonstrated by the recent bombing in London on February 9, 1996, was a protest by the IRA to the arms decommissioning track of the entire peace initiative.

Your students can see the full text of the peace initiative recommendations by accessing the Internet web site on the Mitchell Commission Report:
URL: *http://www.unite.net/customers/alliance/Mitchellrep.html*

20. Sinn Fein and IRA

Sinn Fein (an Irish Gaelic phrase meaning "We Ourselves" and pronounced *sin fin*), the oldest political party in Ireland, has just celebrated its 90th anniversary in 1995. Sinn Fein has been working towards the re-unification of Northern Ireland with the rest of Ireland. The para-military wing of Sinn Fein is the Irish Republican Army. It has been engaged in fierce fighting with British soldiers and the Protestant Irish for years. The recent bombings are reportedly the work of the IRA in its decision to pull out of the peace talks that have been going on since the cease-fire on 31 August, 1994. Sinn Fein says of itself, "Sinn Fein seeks an end to partition which is the cause of conflict, injustice, and division in Ireland." To access the Sinn Fein Home Page, go to:
URL: *http://www.serve.com/rm/sinnfein/index.html*

You can find here:
- Objectives of Sinn Fein stated and how these objectives are hoped to be achieved;
- Link to *An Phoblacht/Republican* newspaper;
- Official documents from Sinn Fein;
- Press releases and news updates;
- Snailmail addresses;
- Opportunity to subscribe to Sinn Fein's Internet mailing list (a small charge);
- Other information

Another site that is pro-Sinn Fein is the Northern Ireland Information Page

URL: *http://www.ireland.com/sinnfein.html*

Find here links to:

- Sinn Fein Web Site;
- *An Phoblacht* (Republican News Online);
- Belfast Telegraph Online;
- Belfast Impressions and Dublin Thought (a list of articles on the issue of the Ireland Troubles);
- All Things Irish (including:
  - The Irish Times Online
  - Irish Web Server Map
  - Irish Music Catalog, articles, playing tips, and much more
  - Access Ireland
  - Croagh Patrick: An Ancient Mountain Pilgrimage
  - Fiddler's Gree
  - The Irish Mall
  - The Online Travel and Entertainment Guide to the best of Ireland
  - Cool Irish WWW Servers
  - Much, much more

21. For a Balanced View of the Irish Question

The Alliance Party of Northern Ireland holds the Unionist point of view, upholding the political and social benefit of maintaining a separate Northern Ireland under British jurisdiction. The Alliance Party is "committed to the creation of a fair, just, peaceful, and prosperous society in Northern Ireland, based on respect for all sections of our community and on the widest possible participation in government and decision making. We are committed to the protecting of human rights, and we utterly oppose the use of violence. We believe that the people of Northern Ireland must decide their own future, and that there should be no change in the constitutional position without their consent."

On Friday, February 9, 1996, a statement from the IRA announced the end of its cease-fire. An hour later, a bomb exploded in the London docklands area. Following the IRA statement, Alliance announced that it was ending direct bilateral contacts with Sinn Fein. A showdown that began on July 1, 1996, between the Orange Order and police adamant in blocking a march through a Roman Catholic neighborhood, renewed fear and tension in Belfast.

For a balanced treatment of the Irish question, please direct your students to access the home page of the Alliance Party of Northern Ireland through the following:

URL: *http://www.unite.net/customers/alliance/index.html*

Included at this site are:

- Alliance information;
- Northern Ireland election facts and figures;
- Other information sources

You may also e-mail the Alliance Party for information, making comments, or asking questions at: *alliance_party@cix.compulink.co.uk*

or

Alliance Party of Northern Ireland,
88 University Street,
Belfast BT7 1HE,
Northern Ireland
Ph. (+44-1232) 324274
Fax (+44-1232) 333147

22. Irish Media News Update

The *Belfast Telegraph* is touted as the only newspaper published in Northern Ireland with widespread readership in all political parties and religious denominations. The paper is in its 126th year of publication and is considered to be the national newspaper of Northern Ireland and one of the leading evening newspapers in the United Kingdom.
URL: *http://www.netcmi.co.uk/beltel/index.html*

Teacher's Notes
A Brief Background of the Troubles in Ireland

The island (or Kingdom) of Ireland has been a single national unit historically. Prior to the Norman invasion from England in 1169, the Irish people were distinct from the people of other kingdoms. They cultivated their own system of law, culture, language, political and social structures. Due to their Celtic cultural background, the Irish people have more in common with the Scots than with the English and the Welsh.

England has colonized Ireland for centuries. During that time, the Irish people have sought to free Ireland from British rule. A series of political and military actions by the Irish nationalist from 1916 to 1920 forced the British government to pass the Government of Ireland Act in 1920 in an effort to partition Northern Ireland from the rest of Ireland. The Act made provision for the creation of two states in Ireland: The Irish Free State, later known as the Republic of Ireland, containing twenty-six of Ireland's thirty-two counties; and Northern Ireland, containing the remaining six counties.

Partition did more than simply divided Ireland physically. It ignited the Civil War of 1922-1923. It also made more acute the divisions between nationalists and unionist in the Six County State, and between the populations of the two states. "The Troubles" is what those who have suffered through them call the 25 years of conflict over whether Northern Ireland should be united with the Republic of Ireland or remain under British rule.

In Northern Ireland itself, an ideological division has arisen. There are those who support the unification of Northern Ireland with the Republic of Ireland. They are known as the republicans or nationalists. Those who wish to remain under British rule are known as unionists or loyalists.

The present-day troubles in Northern Ireland began in 1968 in the city of Derry. The Catholics, who make up two-thirds of the city's population, began to agitate against a town council dominated by Protestants. Following several altercations with the British army, which had been sent in to restore order, the Catholic working-class neighborhood of Bogside became an IRA-controlled zone. The conflict steadily became worse. On 29 January, 1972, nicknamed "Bloody Sunday," the British army opened fire on a civil rights march in Bogside, killing thirteen people. Ever since "bloody Sunday," riots, bombings, snipings, and murders have been common occurrences in certain parts of Northern Ireland, creating a whole generation of urban warriors and shell-shocked civilians. A temporary cease-fire lasted fourteen months, but ended with a renewed effort by the IRA to resume terrorist acts through bombing innocent civilians in London while the peace process was in progress.

"The Orange and the Green"

Oh, it is the biggest mix-up that you have ever seen
My father he was Orange and me mother she was Green.

Oh, my father was an Ulster man, God's Protestant, was he
My mother was a Catholic girl from County Cork was she.
They were married in two churches; lived happily enough
Until the day that I was born and things got rather tough.

Baptized by Father Riley I was rushed away by car
To be made a little Orange man my father's shinin' star.
I was christened David Anthony but still in spite of that,
To my father I was William while my mother called me Pat.

With mother every Sunday, to mass I proudly strolled.
Then after that the Orange Lodge would try to save my soul.
For both sides tried to claim me, but I was smart because
I played the flute or played the harp depending where I was.

One day me Ma's relations came round to visit me
Just as my father's kinfolk were all sitting down to tea.
We tried to smooth things over but they all began to fight
And me being strictly neutral I feist everyone in sight!

Now my parents never could agree about my kind of school.
My learning was undone at home; that's why I'm such a fool.
They both passed on, God rest them, but left me caught between
That awful color problem of the Orange and the Green.

Oh, it is the biggest mix-up that you have ever seen.
My father he was Orange and me mother she was Green.

[A traditional Irish folk song sung by the Irish Rovers]

Excerpts from the "Northern Ireland Peace Book"

The following are some voices of thousands across the miles and at home in Northern Ireland speaking out for a lasting peace in Northern Ireland.

"The peace process must continue for the future of Northern Ireland. Everyone must start to look to the future rather than looking at the past. May peace prevail!" Robert Mulligan, February 27, 1966, Belfast, Antrim, Northern Ireland

"Please let talks replace violence as a form of political expression.... Democracy is the best measure of the people's will...." Simon Adderley, February 27, 1996, Bangor, Wales

"All we are saying is give peace a chance." Sheenagh O'Leary, February 27, 1996, Derry

"17 months of PEACE achieved more than 25 years of WAR. Bring back HOPE. STOP the bombing now." Tim Hortopp, February 27, 1996, Brighton, East Sussex, England

"WHY?" Alona, February 27, 1996, Luxembourg

"Peace and blessings for all, north, south, everywhere. Work together with your kin and friends across the waters and all over the world." Martha Todd-Prather, February 27, 1996, Vancouver, Washington, USA

"I do pray for you that you find the way at last to establish peace for yourselves and your children. It must be just so awful to try and live the terror of attacks, death and destruction. I grieve for your families torn apart, for your children deprived of free laughter and bright futures—and the pain, Oh! the pain you must always feel. It is too much! Please, I pray that you find peace!" Gayle F. Howard. February 26, 1996, Columbus, Ohio, USA

"Don't let the last year-and-a-half go to waste ...." Scott Allison, February 26, 1996, Glasgow, Strathclyde, Scotland

"Peace. An admirable desire anywhere in the world." Trevor Easton, February 26, 1996, Grimsby, Ontario, Canada

"The songs of the people come from the heart. And a people in the midst of war sing of peace." Glade Hoffman, February 25, 1996, Lucerne, CA, USA

"I'd like to think that when my own kids grow up, they don't have to deal with the unbelievable levels of stupidity and blind bigotry that we've faced." Patrick and Neil, February 24, 1996, Belfast, Northern Ireland

"The last two weeks have shown us how fragile the peace process was, but the last eighteen months have shown what is actually possible. We must continue to believe and work together to reclaim peace." Eugene Kearney, February 21, 1996, Meath,

Let's give peace a chance, not only for Northern Ireland, but for all the world! It's time to give the children a chance to grow up. The journey of ten thousand miles begins with the first step. Someone must take that first step." William J. McGinn, February 17, 1996, Shenandoah, PA, USA

Bibliography

Adams, Gerry, *Falls Memories: A Belfast Life*, Roberts Rinehart (Niwot, Colorado), 1994. Adams, president of Sinn Fein, has lived in the Falls Road area of Belfast since his birth in 1948. He recounts the history of this district from its distant past to the present, liberally sprinking his tale with childhood anecdotes. Try retelling some of his adventures to your class.

Bew, Paul and Gordon Gillespie, *Northern Ireland: A Chronology of the Troubles 1968–1993*, Gill and MacMillan (Dublin), 1993. A useful reference book for the teacher and older students during the study of this unit.

Chartres, John et al., *Northern Ireland Scrapbook*, Arms and Armour Press (London), 1986. Over 300 photographs demonstrate what life is like for the Northern Irish in the midst of violence.

Conniff, Richard, "Ireland on Fast-Forward," *National Geographic*, September 1994. Not much has changed in the independent Republic of Ireland. Even Dublin moves at a slower pace than most cities. To the question, "Northern Ireland, will it ever find peace?" the author leaves us hanging. Perhaps instead of joining the rest of Ireland or staying with Britain, it will form its own country. Now there's a twist!

Conroy, John, *Belfast Diary: War as a Way of Life*, Beacon Press (Boston), 1987. The chapter entitled "The Wall and the People Beyond It" tells how the "Peace Wall" came into existence. Conroy lived as a journalist for three years on the Catholic side of the wall but came to know people who lived on both sides. On the flyleaf is a simple map of Belfast showing the location of the Peace Wall.

Levy, Patricia, *Cultures of the World: Ireland*, Marshall Cavendish (New York), 1994. Levy does an excellent job of looking at both the Republic of Ireland and Northern Ireland in an easy flow between the two governments of one culture. Grade 5+.

Lucas, Eileen, *Peace on the Playgroun: Nonviolent Ways of Problem-Solving*, Franklin Watts (New York), 1991. Keeping peace on the playground is the beginning to keeping peace in any country, because those child peacekeepers can become adult peacemakers. Grade 3+.

Lynch, Patricia, "The Three Wishes," *Childcraft: The How and Why Library, Volume 3: Children Everywhere*. Field Enterprises (Chicago), 1975. Paudeen goes with his older brother and sister to hunt for shamrocks. A four-leaf shamrock is said to be lucky and surely they need the food and fuel that luck could bring, but his old grandmother has never known anyone to find one. The Irish twist of speech is delightfully included in the conversations.

Moran, Tom, *A Family in Ireland*, Lerner Publications (New York), 1986. Part of the "Families the World Over" series.

Uris, Jill, *Ireland Revisited*. Doubleday (Garden City, New York), 1982. A book all ages can enjoy; every page is a photograph of the land and her people.

Wall 12: Angel Island: Golden Mountain, Bitter Tears

Pre-Reading Warm-Up

1. Ethnic Communities: A Sociology of Segregation

Anti-Chinese sentiments and actions at the turn of the century in North America forced Chinese immigrants to band together, forming Chinatowns, much like the ghettos where Jews were forced to live in occupied Poland. However, some people feel that today's Chinatowns in North American cities and cities around the world are often more like cultural showcases and social centers for the Chinese people.

As a community study, jointly discover the different ethnic communities, such as Chinatown, Little Italy, French Quarter, Latin Quarter, German Town, and Greek Town, etc., in your city. With the approval of your school administrator, organize a school-bus tour of your city's ethnic communities.

2. An Historical Account: "No. 127, San Francisco Okay"

Mr. Don Wong wrote a touching short story, entitled "No.127, San Francisco Okay," about what happened to 15-year-old Siu Lun Wong in December 1920 at Angel Island. You can read the story by accessing Web site:

URL: *http://www.kqed.org/fromKQED/Cell/Calhist/okay.html*

Print a class set of "No. 127, San Francisco Okay" and study it together as a warm-up activity. Pose the question to your class: What is wrong with saying to a prospective immigrant, "No. 127, San Francisco Okay."? What does that message contain? Discuss.

Language Arts

3. Poetry Appreciation

Select and collect a variety of poems, both classical and modern, that might be appealing to your students. Also ask each student to bring in a poem. Categorize them according to themes. Have them typed up and reproduced as your class anthology. Teach your students to appreciate this collection of poetry through discussing the issues mentioned and/or alluded to and reinforcing their understanding of the poetic devices taught in the previous lesson.

4. Prose vs. Poetry

Explore with your class the differences between prose and poetry. Record the suggested differences in two columns on a sheet of chart paper. As student ideas dwindle, suggest that they consider the form, content, diction, economy of words, and the overall beauty of the genre. Provide ample examples for your students.

5. Wall Poems at Angel Island

Discuss with your students the kinds of subjects and emotions that might have been expressed by Chinese detainees at Angel Island over thirty years between 1910 and 1940. List student responses on a sheet of chart paper.

Contact the The Angel Island Association at (415) 435–3522 for transcripts of the actual wall poems found at the former Immigration Center (now a museum) on Angel island.

6. Poetic Devices

"The Chinese poems carved into the walls of Angel Island were saved by accident.... A park ranger noticed the Chinese writing on the wall and he told people in the Chinese-American community about it."

For thousands of years, Chinese poems have been created on ponderous themes such as parental, filial, conjugal, or patriotic love; grief; personal pain; noble sacrifices; and meaning in life. The language used is often flowery, applying an abundance of poetic devices such as onomatopoeia, metaphor, personification, and rhythmic arrangements, to name a few.

Teach your class the following common poetic devices and provide examples for students to practice through emulation.

Imagery is a picture in words, often made by comparing or associating two different things.

Metaphor is one poetic device used in creating imagery. An example is Tennyson's description of the sea through the eye of an eagle in "The Eagle": "The wrinkled sea beneath him crawls."

Personification is another imagery device with which an event or an inanimate object is given human characteristics, as in the following example: "A naked house, a naked moor,/A shivering pool before the door."

Simile is a third imagery device where one thing is being compared with another using words such as "as" and "like," as in the following examples: "My love is like the red, red rose" and "His broad smile shines like the morning sun."

Diction is the choice of words or figures of speech. The two examples of personification illustrate the poets' choice of words and imageries.

Oxymoron: A poetic device used to emphasize a characteristic or condition with a pair of antithetical words, such as "bitter sweet," "glorious shame," "thunderous silence," and "hauntingly beautiful."

Paradox: A statement that seems contradictory and contains two diametrically opposed conditions, as in "You must die to be born again." and "The king serves his subjects."

Sound effects may be achieved through the use of *onomatopoeia* (a device used to match sound to sense), *alliteration* (the repetition of initial consonant sounds), and *assonance* (the use of similar vowel sounds followed by different consonants). An example of these three sound effect devices can be found in Oliver Herford's poignant poem about the state of our world, entitled *Earth* as shown in an excerpt below:

> "If this little world tonight
> Suddenly should fall through space
> In a hissing, headlong flight,
> Shrivelling from off its face,
> As it falls into the sun...."

"Hissing" is an *onomatopoeia*; "suddenly," "should," and "space" is *alliteration*, so are "hissing" and "headlong"; "tonight" and ""flight" show *assonance*, as do "space" and "face."

Rhythm is the pattern of beat and cadences used to achieve a particular effect which matches and enhances the meaning of the poem, as in a description of a meteor shower by T. Chan:

> "On the dark canvas of Eternity
> He sprinkles sparkling constellations
> And signs His timeless omnipotence
> With shooting stars."

7. Poetry Writing

Introduce free verse (a verse written in lines of irregular rhythm that may or may not rhyme) to your class. This poetic form frees beginning poets from the constraints and mechanics of adhering to a poetic convention, thus providing them with more technical freedom in creating.

Ask your students to suggest a list of topics for poems. They might begin with those with which they are most familiar and comfortable, such as "My Grandmother," "Summer Cottage," "My Pal, the Computer," "Rowland, My Dog," etc. In a follow-up lesson, suggest to them topics that are social commentaries, such as "The Next Millennium," "Technocrats," "Big Brother's Still Watching," "How to Kill the Earth: Let Me Count the Ways," etc.

Encourage the use of poetic devices throughout the writing process. Invite and encourage students to share their poems. Provide students with choices to share or to pass because some individuals may be sensitive to sharing their feelings on particular subjects.

8. Imitate the Chinese Style of Poetry

Chinese poetry is written with flowery language, exaggerated emotions, and an appeal to the nobler character of man. Provide your students with an example of a Chinese poem, and assign them to write one that imitates the emotiveness and stylistic characteristics. The following Chinese poem, entitled "Elegy," written in the early 1900s by Tsui Chee More and translated by T. Chan, serves as an example. Explore with your class the meaning(s) and emotions of the poem.

Elegy

When I am dead, my dear,
Don't chant me elegies;
My grave needs no cinnamonrose,
Nor the shades of pine trees.
Allow the emerald-green grass above me
To be baptized with raindrops,
Jeweled with morning dew.

If you wish ...
Please house me in your memories,
But, if you wish not to remember me,
Ne'er could I marvel the freshness of the meadows,
Nor taste the honey-drops of rain,
Nor hear the nocturnal wailing
Of the nightingale again.

In the unending twilight of indecisions,
When the sun neither rises nor sets,
Maybe ...
Maybe you are in my memories,
But again, maybe not.

9. Empathy with Human Agonies and Indignities

"These poems were written by Chinese immigrants who were lonely and angry."

As an extension learning activity, ask students to compare the respective fears, agonies, and emotions of the Jewish prisoners held in concentration camps, those of native North Americans who were forced to move onto reservations, and those of the Chinese immigrants detained at Angel Island as a result of a racist immigration policy. Explore with your class other modern-day holocausts and Angel Island-type human rights violations as a result of racism found at home and around the world.

10. Creative Writing (A)

Ask your class to pretend that they are Chinese immigrants who have been detained for over half-a-year at the Immigration Center on Angel Island in 1925. They have been given grueling interrogations to qualify for immigration. Ask them to write home about their sea voyage from China to the "Golden

Mountain," their reception when they landed, their experiences while being detained against their will at Angel Island, the kinds of questions they were asked, their pains, fears, and hopes.

After some research, students could do a similar creative-writing project about the Ellis Island immigrants.

11. Creative Writing (B)

Ask your class to pretend that they are Chinese laborers working in California in the 1880s. Ask them to write home to their loved ones in China describing the daily back-breaking work, the discrimination they receive from Americans, and their painfully lonely existence.

12. Creative Writing (C)

As a creative writing task, ask each student to pretend he or she is the president of the country in the 1880s.

A) Ask your students to write about directions they would have taken for shaping immigration, social, economic, and foreign policies if they were the president of the country in the 1880s.

B) What would they have said to the detainees on Angel Island?

C) Now ask your students to pretend they are the president today. How would they shape immigration policy?

Social Studies

13. History of Immigration

"They were lonely because they missed their families in China and they were angry because they knew they were being held against their will at Angel Island...."

For thirty years (1910-1940), Angel Island served as a point of entry to the United States for many immigrant groups. However, it also served to enforce the Chinese Exclusion Act signed by President Hayes in 1882 to deny entry to Chinese only. No other group was denied entry to the USA before or after. Thus, the Immigration Center at Angel Island became a detention center for hundreds of Chinese immigrants who were forced to undergo a formidable interrogation process. If successful, the Chinese were permitted to go and live in San Francisco. If not, they were forced to returned to China. The detainees were kept on Angel Island from an average of two weeks to the longest recorded detention of 22 months.

The objective of this exercise is to acquaint ourselves with the history of immigration and to pose the rhetorical question: "Who belongs here?" Assign your class a research project on the history of immigration policies in our country. Ask them to make a comparative study of the two immigration reception centers, Ellis Island in the East and Angel Island in the West, in the U.S.

Who Belongs Here?, a modern-day true story of a young refugee, written by the author of *Talking Walls*, Margy Burns Knight, and published by Tilbury House, Publishers in 1993, provides a wealth of ideas for discussion on the topic of immigration. The *Teacher's Guide* for *Who Belongs Here?* offers many practical teaching ideas on issues of racism, multiculturalism, human rights, and immigration.

14. "Who Belongs Here?"—An Exercise on our Cultural Mosaic

Survey your students as to the countries of origin of their families. Give them a day or two to make enquiries from their parents or relatives. Place on a sheet of chart paper the countries of origin of your students and the number of families from the same places. Ask students to graphically represent this data. They may use pie graphs, bar graphs, charts, line graphs, etc.

Post the finished graphs on the classroom walls. Allow students an opportunity to digest the information and to raise questions about the heritage composition of your class. Pose the question: "Whose ancestry was indigenous or aboriginal to this country?" Lead a discussion on how the USA and Canada are made up of peoples of diverse origins and cultures. Also discuss why some groups are/were treated differently than others?

15. Public and State-Led Racism

The European Jews and the Chinese in America had plenty in common. Both Germans and Californians found easy scapegoats for their respective economic downturns: the Jews in Europe and the Chinese immigrants in the U.S. In both instances, public discrimination and maltreatment of targeted groups were legitimized by the actions of their governments. The Nazi government spearheaded the persecution and murder of the Jews, while the U.S. government passed racist laws to deny entry to Chinese immigrants and violate the civil rights of those who were already living and working in the U.S.

As more and more Chinese immigrants came and offered cheap labor in the New World, white laborers and politicians began to blame the Chinese for the economic problems in California. Anti-Chinese sentiments were expressed openly through demonstrations, harassment, violence, and unjust legislation.

On March 4, 1882, California Governor George C. Perkins actually declared a legal holiday for anti-Chinese demonstrations. The anti-Chinese campaign reached a high point with the Chinese Exclusion Act of 1882, signed by President Hayes to deny Chinese entry to the U.S. Chinese, like native North Americans and African-Americans, were prohibited from testifying against whites, and their children were sent to segregated schools.

The Immigration Center on Angel Island was opened in 1910 to process immigrant groups and detain Chinese immigrants through tortuous and lengthy interrogations. When the Chinese Exclusion Act was finally repealed on December 18, 1943, the Chinese immigration quota was limited to 105 people each year, as opposed to the quota of 60,000 for people from Britain.

Discuss with your students how people and even governments might be misguided to discriminate against minority groups. Brainstorm other examples of similar shameful events, in the past or at the present, around the world.

16. Confronting the "-isms" in Our Society

Not only are people of different racial, cultural, linguistic, and religious backgrounds often being discriminated against (racism), different genders (sexism), people of different age groups (agism), people who are devoted to different systems of belief (sectarianism or parochialism), people who are concerned exclusively with local matters, (provincialism), people of different socio-economic status (classism or elitism), people of different sexual orientations, and handicapped people are routinely discriminated against and unfairly treated in many instances.

Survey how many of your students have experienced discrimination and prejudice just because they are children or youths. Invite students to offer examples from real life. Discuss with them the existence of all kinds of "-isms" in our society. Explore with them the possible origins of those fears and discriminations and how we, as a society, become more tolerant with and accepting of differences.

17. Education of the Young: Segregation or Integration?

Segregation in education happened (and is happening) in many places, both at home and abroad. Until 1954, black students were segregated from the whites in many schools in the U.S. In the 1880s, Chinese children received segregated education in California. The first community-operated Chinese school was established in 1884 in San Francisco. In response to the negative attitudes and discriminatory laws in the U.S., those early Chinese schools taught a complete Chinese curriculum in preparation for the children's eventual return to China.

Even today, children learn in segregated environments due to a multitude of reasons. As reported on February 24, 1996 in a news article by Associated Press, the blacks in South Africa are still feeling the last gasp of apartheid as whites challenge integrated schools in Potgietersrus. Hong Kong, a British Crown Colony, still boasts segregated elitist schools for wealthy European children only. Very few jurisdictions embrace the concept and practice of mainstream education for the physically and intellectually challenged. Children with special needs are still taught in segregated settings, apart from the mainstream.

Lead your class in discussing the merits and shortcomings of segregated education, be it racial, linguistic, ability-based, political, or socio-economic in nature. After the class discussion, assign students to write an essay on the topic.

Science

18. Bridge Engineering

When we think of San Francisco today, we think "Golden Gate Bridge." Though not finished until 1937, when Angel Island as an entry point for immigrants was nearing closure, many immigrants would have watched its construction with interest. They would never have seen such a project in their homeland. Lead your students on a study of bridges: what kinds there are, what difficulties the builders have, how bridges are built, and what some of the famous bridges of the world are. After or during your study, visit some of the bridges in your community and evaluate them based on what the students have learned in their research.

19. Gunpowder: A Chinese Invention

The Chinese are credited with the invention of gunpowder, which they first used for fireworks and later to propel rockets against the Mongols in the 1232 war. Gunpowder, still used today for fireworks, blank cartridges, and some blasting, is made of a combination of potassium nitrate, charcoal, and sulfur. Have some of your students research the history of gun powder, some find what explosive techniques have replaced gunpowder, and others examine the anatomy of modern-day fireworks (as well as how the wonderful designs and colors are achieved).

Mathematics

20. Chinese Abacus—A Hands-On Experience

The abacus is a calculating device, probably of Babylonian origin, that has enjoyed a historic importance in commerce in China and a reputation of being the precursor of the modern calculator and the computer. While there is no actual record of the origin of the abacus, it is described in a Chinese book written in the Yuan Dynasty (14th century).

The abacus can be used for addition, subtraction, multiplication, and division; for whole numbers as well as fractions; and for finding square and cubed roots. For someone who is conversant with using the instrument, the act of calculation can be extraordinarily speedy and accurate. A story goes that two professors entered a speed calculation contest. One used the computer, and the other the abacus, to solve a complex mathematical problem. As the legend spins, the abacus-user beat the computer-user in plenty of time.

The Chinese abacus (*suan-puan*) has a center, horizontal bar with vertical columns of two beads above the bar and five beads below. (See the illustration on page 111.) Each of the beads above the bar represents five units. Each bead below the bar represents one unit. Each vertical column of beads represents a different "place value", with the ones on the extreme right hand side of the frame, working through the tens, the hundreds, the thousands, ten thousands, the hundred thousands, the millions, ten millions and so on. In calculations, the beads must be pushed against the center bar to be counted. All beads begin as far from the center bar as possible. This indicates the number "0."

To show the number 1: Move 1 bead on the ones column from below the horizontal bar to the central bar.

To show the number 5: Move 5 beads on the same column in the same way. However, you do not want all the beads from one column pushed up to the bar at the same time, so you move all 5 back down and instead, move 1 bead from above the bar down to the bar. This indicates 5 .

Ten: The 2 beads on the ones column that are above the bar move down to the bar. But we have the same situation as with 5—all the beads are now against the central bar and we don't want that. Move the 2 beads back, away from the center and move up 1 bead from the next column (the tens) from below the bar, up to the bar.

Twelve: Keep the 10 bead against the central bar and move 2 beads on the ones column from below the bar up to the bar.

Eighteen: The "one" bead in the tens column stays in the same place as it was with 10 and 12. However, on the ones column, you need one "five" bead from above the bar to come down to the bar and three "one" beads from below the bar to come up to the bar.

Twenty: Two beads on the tens column from below the bar come up to the bar.

Four hundred and sixty-three: On the ones column, raise 3 "one" beads up to the bar; on the tens column, raise 1 "one" bead up to the bar and 1 "five" bead down to the bar; on the hundreds column, raise 4 "one" beads up to the bar.

2 + 2: First show 2 on the abacus (2 "one" beads on the ones column are raised to the bar). Now add 2 more, or raise 2 more beads on the same column to join the first 2 beads. You should have four "one" beads raised to the bar on the ones column. This addition is very easy and straightforward. Try the next.

2 + 3: This isn't too hard yet. Start with the 2. Now add the three, but because you don't want all the beads in one column all at the bar, you must push all 5 beads away from the bar and bring down the next larger bead which is a "five" bead on the same column.

2 + 6: Start with the 2. You can't bring up 6 "one" beads, because there aren't that many, so you know automatically that you need the "five" bead from above the bar. Bring that down to the bar and add 1 "one" bead from below. You should have 3 "one" beads and 1 "five" bead against the center bar on the ones column. This equals 8.

8 + 8: Start with the 8. Now bring down 1 "five" bead in the ones column. But you don't want all the beads against the bar, so raise both "five" beads away from the bar and bring to the bar the next largest bead which happens to be a "one" bead on the tens column. However, you have only added 5 so far; you need to add another 3. Going back to the ones column, you see you can't raise 3 more "one" beads. Raise to the bar what you can, 2 "one" beads. Now you have 5 "one" beads at the bar, but you don't want all the beads at the bar at one time so you lower them away from the bar and bring down 1 "five" bead. You can now add the last 1 by raising a "one" bead on the ones column. You should show: 1 "one" bead on the tens column; 1 "five" bead on the ones column and 1 "one" bead on the ones column which equals 16.

This all sounds cumbersome at first, but it is not really. After some experience you develop a rhythm. Walking into a Hong Kong accounting office twenty-five years ago was a noisy experience, since the bookkeepers kept their abacuses clacking constantly. After you have developed some comfort with displaying numbers and adding them (try other numbers and addition sentences), try subtraction. To subtract numbers, just push the number of beads away from the center bar, breaking the fives into ones and the tens into fives.

Arrange to bring to class an abacus for your students to look at and handle. You can buy one in a Chinatown store. Show students how to use it by placing it on the overhead projector as you manipulate the beads in the process of calculating. You can also use student-made abacuses. See "Arts and Crafts" in this chapter.

21. A Mathematics Activity in Data Management

From official records, the data on the population of Chinese in California is as follows:

1848 - 54
1851 - 4,000
1852 - 25,000 (largest minority in California)
1860 - 35,000 (70% were miners)
1870 - 50,000 (Depression in California)
1880 - 75,218 (Total of Chinese in the U.S. was 105,465)
1882 - Chinese Exclusion Act
1890 - 72,472
1892 - Geary Act extended and reinforced the Exclusion Act
1900 - 45,000
1920 - 27,000
1950 - 50,000
1990 - 704,850

Assign groups of students to construct graphical representations of the above data on population of Chinese in California throughout the past 150 years. Charts, picto-graphs, bar graphs, line graphs, and pie graphs, etc. may be used.

Post the data representations on the board. Lead a discussion as to why the Chinese population fluctuated over the past 150 years in California.

Arts and Crafts

22. Make an Abacus

As a hands-on arts-and-crafts experience, assist your students in making their own home-spun abacuses. The materials you need are either free or cheap, suitable for teaching innovatively on a shoe-string budget.

Materials:
A class set of personal-sized pizza boxes. (Call up your local pizza restaurant and request 30 personal-sized pizza boxes. Tell them the purpose of your request. They usually are happy to oblige.)
A spool of coarse fishing line
Small red and white beads (plastic or wood); or salad macaroni (some to be dyed with red food coloring) would do.

Method:
1. Cut off the top of the pizza box carefully with a razor blade.
2. Divide the length of the box side into eight equal parts and mark the divisions on the top and bottom sides of the box.
3. Next, divide the vertical sides of the box into eight equal parts again and mark down the divisions on the sides of the box.
4. At the second mark from the top of the box, attach, with tape, a strip of cardboard (made from the box top) the same depth as the sides of the box. This will be the center bar of your abacus, situated at the top quarter of the box.
5. Use a pin to poke eight holes at the markings on both the upper and lower sides of the box as well as those marked on the center bar.
6. Cut fishing line into appropriate lengths and make a knot at the top of the box.
7. Place two white beads through the fishing line in front of the center bar, then loop the line through the hole in the center bar.

8. Next, place five red beads through the line before tying a knot at the bottom hole. Now you have the first row of beads strung. If you do it from right to left, then, the one's place value line is complete.

9. Continue the same process with the rest of the place value lines on the abacus. When all eight lines are strung with two white beads above the center bar and five red beads below, you will have manufactured your own abacus for arithmetic calculation.

The Abacus

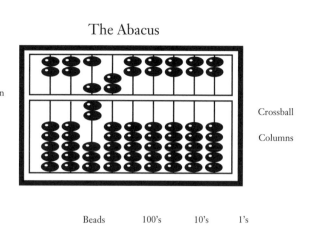

Heaven

Crossball

Columns

Earth

Frame   Beads   100's   10's   1's

Food Experience

23. Recipe

The Chinese do not, as a rule, eat dessert after their meals. However, desserts can be found on the menu of Dim Sum, a mid-day meal served at special restaurants which specialize in individualized packets of food such as egg rolls, steamed buns, etc. This dessert is simple to make, is safe for the students because it does not involve cooking, and is a favorite among children.

Almond Delight: A Chinese Dessert

Ingredients:
2 packets (or 2 tablespoons) unflavored gelatin
1 3/4 cups of cold water
1 1/2 cups of evaporated milk
2 teaspoons almond extract
1/2 cup white sugar
2 8-ounce cans of Mandarin orange sections undrained.

Method:
1. Soak gelatin in 1/2 cup of cold water for 5 min..
2. Bring the remaining 1 1/4 cup water to a boil and add to the soaked gelatin.
3. Stir until the mixture is thoroughly dissolved.
4. Stir in milk, almond extract, and sugar.
5. Pour the mixture into a 9" by 12" pan.
6. Place dish in fridge for 3 or 4 hours, until the gelatin is firmly set.
7. Using a sharp knife, cut the gelatin into 1/2" squares (which will result in the gelatin being cubed when removed from the pan).
8. To serve, lift portions of the gelatin into individual dishes and top with the oranges and the accompanying liquid.

Note: you may substitute canned fruit cocktail for the oranges.

Internet Resources

24. Angel Island—Ellis Island of the West

This is an Internet site just for the study of Angel Island. You will find it at:
URL: *http://www.kqed.org/fromKQED/Cell/Calhist/angel.html*

Look for:

- Angel Island history;
- *No. 127, San Francisco, Okay,* a story;
- Instructions to make a story board (easy enough for primary grades);
- Educational extension activities;
- A written walking tour of San Francisco's Chinatown (no photos, but an interesting description of many sites, revealing the Asian heritage of this neighborhood, even if you live too far away to actually visit it in person).

25. Golden Legacy Curriculum

The Chinese Historical and Cultural Project (CHCP), based in Santa Clara County, California, is a non-profit organization founded to promote and preserve Chinese and Chinese-American history and culture through community outreach activities.

The CHCP has produced *The Golden Legacy Curriculum,* an award-winning (Santa Clara County Reading Council Award, 1994) multimedia curriculum with a teacher's guide, for the third, fourth, and fifth grades, focusing on the Chinese people and their culture. The curriculum includes lesson plans, hands-on activities, 20 color slides, and a video entitled *"Home Base: A Chinatown called Heinlenville."* Not all this is available on the Internet; some must be ordered (see address below). To access the lesson plans, information, and activities, however, go to:

URL: *http://www.kqed.org/fromKQED/Cell/golden/glmenu.html*

The Golden Legacy covers the following curriculum topics with detailed lesson plans and hands-on learning activities:

- New Beginnings: Immigration and Chinatown;
- Survival: Railroad Building, New Almaden Mine, and Agriculture;
- Daily Life: Clothing, Bound Feet, Queues, Value System, and Names;
- Traditions: Lunar Calendar, Celebrations, and Symbolism;
- Education System: Writing System, Abacus, Tangram, Folk Tales, Songs, Games, and Puppetry;
- Lasting Legacy: Postage Stamps and Conclusion.

For further information about the *Golden Legacy Curriculum,* please use e-mail addresses: *rutledge@dnai.com* or *jochim@sjsuvm1.sjsu.edu*
For information about the video, *"Home Base: A Chinatown Called Heinlenville,"* please call the Chinese Historical and Cultural Project at (408) 735-9417.

Community Resources

26. An Excursion to the Museum of Immigration on Angel Island

For schools that are in the San Francisco area, it would be exciting to organize a one-day excursion or a two-day camping trip to the former Immigration Center, now a museum, on Angel Island. If possible, arrange for a guided tour of the former detention center where so many Chinese immigrants wasted their precious lives away, waiting to be "processed." Students will be thrilled to see, with their own eyes, the very heart-breaking poems carved and penned on the walls of the Center. Invite a Chinese parent or friend to go along, so that poems and writings may be translated on the spot. Bring with you a 35 mm camera or a camcorder to film the wall poems. For more information, call (415) 435–1915.

Bibliography

Carlisle, Norman and Madelyn, "The True Book of Bridges," *I Want to Know About....* Childrens Press (Chicago), 1972. Look with your young students at how bridges began, what they were like, different kinds of bridges and how bridges are built.

Growing up with Science: The Illustrated Encyclopedia of Invention, Volume 6. H.S. Stuttman (Westport, Connecticut), 1984. "Explosives," and "Fireworks and Flares" in vol. 6 and "Gunpowder" in vol. 23 are three articles that can assist the students in their science research.

Haskins, Jim, *Count Your Way Through China*, Carolrhoda Books (Minneapolis), 1987. Count to 10 in Chinese, learning about 4 important animals of myth, 5-toned instruments, and the 10 major dynasties. Grade 1+.

Kalman, Bobbie, *China; The People*, Crabtree Publishing Company (New York), 1989. Bobbie Kalman is prolific in producing usable books for the elementary classroom. This one is no exception. Grade 4+.

Knight, Margy Burns, *Who Belongs Here? An American Story*, Tilbury House, Publishers (Gardiner, ME), 1993. While this book tells the story of a young Cambodian immigrant and the discrimination he faces, it also traces the history of immigration in the United States and builds empathy for recent immigrants.

Lip, Evelyn, *Out of China: Culture and Traditions*, Addison-Wesley (Reading, Massachusetts), 1993. What a great book! Chinese writing, architecture (including furniture), cleebrations, beliefs, and much more is included with detail and excellent illustrations that will intrigue intermediate students.

Takaki, Ron, *Journey to the Golden Mountain*, Chelsea House (New York) 1996. The story of the first immigrants from China to the United States.

"Where Am I?" *The Young Children's Encyclopedia, Volume 14.* Encyclopaedia Britannica Inc. (Chicago), 1977. Read the clues and see if your young students can guess that this description fits San Francisco.

Yee, Paul, *The Curses of Third Uncle*, James Lorimer (Toronto), 1986. Fourteen-year-old Lillian lives in Vancouver in the early 1900s. Her father has disappezred and Third Uncle threatens to send Lillian, her mother,and her sisters back to China. Lillian must find her father to save her family. Grade 4+.

Yee, Paul, *Roses Sing on a New Snow: A Delicious Tale*, Macmillan (New York), 1991. This story depicts the customs and traditions of family life in Chinatown during the early 1900s. Grade 4+.

Yee, Paul, *Tales from Golden Mountain: Stories of the Chinese in the New World*, Macmillan (New York), 1989. Very short stories, with a full-page painting to illustrate each one. Even grade 1 students will enjoy having these stories read to them.

Yee, Paul, *Teach Me to Fly, Skyfighter! and Other Stories*, James Lorimer (Toronto), 1983. Sharon and her family have moved to Vancouver Chinatown from Vancouver Island. Like many Canadian-born Chinese, she doesn't understand the Chinese language as well as her China-born, grade 5 classmates. Although she looks the same, she's determined to prove she's different. Grade 4+.

Yep, Laurence, *Dragonwings*, HarperCollins (New York), 1975. This adventure story portrays early 20th-century San Francisco from the point of view of Chinese immigrants.

Yung, Judy, *Unbound Feet: A Social History of Chinese Women in San Francisco*, University of California Press (Berkeley), 1995. Of interest to teachers or advanced students.

Wall 13   Pablo Neruda: Poet Laureate In Exile

Pre-Reading Warm-Up

1. Pen Names

"...he took the pen name Pablo Neruda. He chose Neruda after one of his favorite Czechoslovakian poets.

Pablo Neruda (1904-1973) was born Ricardo Eliecer Neftali Reyes y Basoalto in Chile. He won a Nobel Prize in Literature in 1971. Explore with your class the reasons why pseudonyms are used (pen names by some writers and acting names by some actors, etc.). Ask the students if they know if any famous people who use pseudonyms. Then ask them to write pseudonyms for themselves.

Language Arts

2. Letter Writing

The Chilean government is now very proud of Pablo Neruda. Encourage your class to write to the following places for more information on the very colorful life of this Nobel Laureate.

In the U.S. A.
Embassy of the Republic of Chile,
1732 Massachusetts Avenue, NW,
Washington, DC 20036
USA
Ph. (202) 785-1746; Fax (202) 887-5579

In Canada
Embassy of the Republic of Chile,
151 Slater Street, Suite 605,
Ottawa, Ontario
Canada, K1P 5H3
Ph. (613) 235-4402; Fax (613) 235-1176

In Chile
Servicio Nacional de Turismo -
   SERNATUR,
Avda Providencia 1550,
Casilla 14082, Santiago
Chile
Ph. (2) 236-0531

Ana Maria Diaz Grez, Director
Fundacion Pablo Neruda
Santiago,
Chile
e-mail/fax: fundacio.npab1001@chilnet.cl

3. An Audiovisual Approach to Poetry—An Award-Winning Teaching Innovation

This poetry teaching idea won national recognition for Thomas V. Chan in 1977. The Hilroy Fellowship Award for Innovative Teaching was juried by the Canadian Federation of Teachers. The following is a tried-and-true method of facilitating a love for poetry in young people.

Objective

The purpose of this approach to poetry is to bring about greater enjoyment to students in appreciating and writing poetry. With appropriate modifications, the approach and the accompanying techniques may be used to teach poetry to students from K to 12.

Rationale

Since children come from different cultural and socio-economic backgrounds, their values, life experiences, points of view, and levels of maturity are very diverse. When presented with the art form of poetry, children's reactions may range from a complete void of identification on the one hand, to a total emotional and intellectual empathy on the other. The use of the twin stimuli of sight and sound as motivators and supplements to poetry appreciation helps to evoke empathetic reactions from children to the art form in accordance with their respective experiential, emotional, spiritual, and intellectual capacities.

Method:

A poem generally has a central theme. Contributing to the theme are specific ideas which are found throughout the poem. These specific ideas are referred to as "meaningful units" as they lend meanings to the poem. A "meaningful unit" may be a key word, a phrase, a figure of speech, a line, or even a stanza. To visually interpret a poem, one matches the "meaningful units" with mental pictures that come to mind (imageries). Employing the matching technique, a student may interpret a poem by producing, for instance, a slide/tape or a video presentation. Conversely, he may create his own poetry in response to audiovisual stimulation.

Procedure:

This approach requires a unit on poetry that lasts approximately four to five weeks, and it is a three-pronged operation.

A) *Operation One:* The first week is spent in appreciating poems with which the teacher has already matched visuals (color slides or pictures) and sounds (music, sound effects, and/or oral readings). The poems are discussed in light of the images selected. By the end of the first week, the students should have a working familiarity with the approach.

B) *Operation Two:* Students are engaged in group projects which involve imagery interpretations of poems of their own choice. They learn to ascribe literal as well as symbolic meanings to their interpretations. Audiovisual productions of the poems are the end-products of the creative process. A day is set aside for the presentation of their finished products.

C) *Operation Three:* While the projects are being undertaken as take-home assignments, the third operation takes place in the classroom. This time, the stimulation process is reversed. Slides and music are used and students are asked to react to them creatively. Poetic form and conventions are de-emphasized. Students are encouraged to write in any form they like best. Within the three weeks during which the groups are producing their audiovisual interpretations of poems, operations one and three interchange from time to time to offer a variety of activities. As the students' interest levels in poetry become high, they will have little difficulty in enjoying poems without the use of audiovisuals.

Poetry Scripting

Please find below a sample poetry scripting form. It's called the scripting board because it is not too dissimilar to story boards used in movie scripting. To assist students in scripting a poem, ask them to read the poem several times and seek to identify the central theme of the poem.

As they read the poem again, ask them to take notice of particular words, phrases, lines, stanzas, or poetic devices that help create pictures in their minds. These imagery-evoking elements are coined by the author as "meaningful units" as they lend meaning to the main theme. Students write down on the poetry scripting board the meaningful units in one column and what they visualize as their pictorial representation, literal or figurative, on the second column.

When the process of mental visualization is complete, so will be the scripting of the poem. The next phase is for students, in working pairs, to produce audio-visual shows on the poems they have chosen. Slide shows, videos, and cut-and-paste poetry project books are all acceptable formats. They may enjoy playing a musical soundtrack as background to the show / presentation. Set aside several lessons for students to show their productions. Provide your class with a set of criteria with which each production is judged according to its literary and artistic merits.

Organize an evening of "The Academy Awards of Poetic Arts" for the parents of your students. Invite your administrator and colleagues to attend. Train a couple of M.C.'s for this event. Make it a gala event by presenting recognitions to working teams in such categories as: The Best Photography

Award, The Best Musical Background Award, The Best Poetic Interpretation Award, The Best Team Players Award, The Best Effort Award, The Most Original Award, etc. Your students, their parents, and your colleagues will be pleased with the effort and quality of student work. Have fun!

Poetry Scripting Board

Meaningful Units In Poem   *Imageries In Visuals*

_____

_____

_____

_____

_____

_____

Social Studies

4. Chile: A Country at "Land's End"

Pablo Neruda was born in 1904 in a small town in southern Chile. Chile is an oddly shaped country stretching along a narrow strip of land in the southwestern-most corner of the continent, nestled between the Andes mountains and the Pacific Ocean. This geographic remoteness might have given rise to a story behind the origin of the country's name: Chilli, which means "where the land ends" in an aboriginal language.

Two places of interest are the Easter Islands (famous for mysterious huge stone sculptures) and the Juan Fernandez Archipelago (where the story of a marooned sailor inspired Daniel Dafoe to write *The Adventures of Robinson Crusoe*).

As a social studies project, help your students research Chile: its land, history, and people. Besides library research, encourage them to contact the local Chilean community for interviews and Chilean tourism organizations for informational brochures. As a special focus, ask students to include research on either the Easter Islands or the Juan Fernandez Archipelago. Invite people into your classroom who have visited Chile.

5. Contemporary World Affairs

"Neruda didn't like it when a military government took over his country on September 11, 1973. A few weeks later he died, and the new military leader warned people to stay away from Neruda's home."

Chile is one of the oldest democracies in the Americas. However, it has had its share of civil strife. In 1973, a coup d'état brought about the lengthy rule of a military government which lasted until 1990. Pablo Neruda spent the last few months of his life speaking out for democracy and human rights.

Assign an essay for students to research the dark days of the seventeen years of military government in Chile. (See the bibliography at the end of this chapter.) Students could pair up and each cover a year or other segment of time, and then their work could be linked together and presented as a T.V. documentary or news hour.

6. Alfred Nobel and the Nobel Foundation: A Research Project

Chile is the only Latin American nation to be home to two Nobel Laureates in Literature: Gabriela Mistral and Pablo Neruda.

The Nobel Prize is such an extraordinary recognition that winners of the Prize quickly rise to international fame. The Nobel Prize is awarded annually by the Nobel Foundation in Stockholm, Sweden, for those who make great contributions to mankind in the endeavors of physics, chemistry, physiology or medicine, literature, economics, and peace.

The famed Prize for excellence was the brainchild and legacy of one remarkable Swede, Alfred

Nobel, himself an accomplished scientist, inventor, industrialist, and humanitarian. Assign students a research paper on the life and times of this interesting humanitarian. (Please refer to the "Teacher's Notes" of this chapter for a brief biography of Alfred Nobel.)

As an extension activity, your students may conduct a search for names and details of every Nobel Laureate since 1905. The Nobel Foundation offers an on-line Directory of Laureates. The URL is:

http://www.nobel.se/cgi-bin/uncgi/nobel?to=5&lng=0&bkp=4&ctr=1&picb=0&gfx=1

The mailing address of the office of the Nobel Foundation is:

Box 5232, S-102 45

Stockholm, Sweden

The e-mail address for the Foundation is: *webmaster@www.nobel.se*

Science

7. The Desert

Chile has the driest desert on earth. Young students can do a simple study on the desert, learning what a desert is, what animals, plants, and people live in deserts, and where in the world the major deserts are located. An excellent resource for beginning readers is *The True Book of Deserts* by Elsa Posel (see the bibliography at the end of this chapter).

8. Ocean: Tsunamis (Tidal Waves)

Tsunamis are not tidal at all but are triggered by earthquakes and volcanic explosions. Chile, though not the worst country hit by these destructive waves, is vulnerable to tsunamis perhaps because of its very long coastline on the ring of fire (it also experiences more than its fair share of earthquakes and volcanic eruptions). Provide your students with reference material and books that will help them learn more about this uncontrollable menace to mankind. Where do tsunami come from? Where do they occur? How fast do they travel? What are the hazards? What are some real-life stories of places hit by tsunami? See "Tsunami" in the bibliography for more information on this quirk of nature.

9. The Ocean: Fishing

Chile is dominated by the Pacific coast on her 2,700-mile (4,350 km) eastern boundary (that doesn't count the bays, that's just stretching a ruler, if you will, from the northern border to the southern tip). With most of the land mountainous, no one is far from the ocean in Chile.

One activity common to nearly all coastal countries around the world is fishing. No longer, however, are fisherman content to cast handmade nets over the sides of their boats. Instead, technology has advanced this occupation to the place where a knowledge of science is a real boon. Computers and sonar waves transmit information on the position and depth of fish near the boat. Factory ships head for sea and don't return for months, flash freezing or canning their catch immediately, resulting in a fresher product for the market. Some of the students in your class may be interested in pursuing this topic further. They can examine navigational, locating, and catching techniques used by commercial fishermen around the world. See "Fishing Industry" in the bibliography at the end of this chapter.

Mathematics

10. Measurement—Linear

Chile is the seventh largest nation in South America. It is more than double the size of Italy and almost one-and-a-half times that of Spain. The distance between Arica, the northernmost city, and Puerto Williams, the southernmost town in the country, is 2,609 miles (4,200 kilometers). This is the same distance as between San Francisco and New York.

Provide students with a map of Chile. Ask them to measure with a string and calculate, with reference to map scale, the distance between the northern and southern end of the country in miles or kilometers. Mark on the string with a red marker the two points that represent the two geographical extremities of Chile.

Ask students to use the two red marks on the string to mark off major cities in your country. Ask students to locate at least five pairs of cities whose distance from each other is the same as the length of Chile. Notate this data in project books.

11. Measurement—Area

Provide your class with sheets of tracing paper. Ask students to lightly trace out the outline of Chile from the map in the atlas. Have them estimate which other country (or countries) and/or state(s) is close in area to that of Chile. This requires students to visualize geometric shapes and practice their spatial relationships.

Direct students to check out their estimations by cutting up their traced outlines of Chile and placing the geometric shapes on the maps (to the same scale) of their chosen countries. Now, they have a more accurate visual check of their estimations. Or, if you prefer, they can check their answers with an encyclopedia year book (which will list areas for each country).

12. Data Management—Graphing Population

Chile is a country with a youthful population, nearly 50 % of whom are under 25 years of age, an interesting statistic that will make an impact on the world scene by the year 2001.

Ask students what the information that appears below tells them about Chile's population distribution by age group. Instruct them to represent the information in the form of a chart or a graph.

Chile's Population Distribution by Age Group (1992 census)

Ages	0 - 14	29.4 %
Ages	15 - 24	18.2 %
Ages	25 - 39	24.6 %
Ages	40 - 49	10.6 %
Ages	50 - 64	10.6 %
Ages	65+	6.6 %

Assign students to look up, from federal census records, the population distribution by age in your country. They can graph the data and compare it with that of Chile. From the information they have gathered on our country's age-specific distribution of people, what conclusions can they draw? Discuss.

Arts and Crafts

13. Build a Fence

Needed:
Fence pickets (one for each person in your class or, if your class is very large, one per two people in the class)
1x4 planks (enough to extend twice the length of the fence you are building)
Nails
Hammers (students can bring their own)
Newspapers or "drop cloth"
White latex paint
Paint brushes (students can bring their own)
Pencils, pens, markers, etc.
Directions:
1. Lay the 1x4s on the ground in two parallel lines far enough apart that the pickets will extend

beyond, 4-6 inches (10-15 cm), at the top and bottom of the fence.

2. Lay the pickets, perpendicularly, on top of the 1x4s, allowing each student, or pair of students, to nail their picket on before the next picket is laid.

3. Spread newspapers or other protection under the fence and paint.

4. When the paint has dried, each student can write one or more poems or tributes to Neruda (or to other poets, or to him- or herself) on his or her picket.

5. Find a place to display your masterpiece.

14. A Three-Dimensional Map of South America:

To assist students in becoming familiar with the continent of South America and its countries, try the following hands-on learning experience.

Lesson 1:

Provide students with atlases and mimeographed outline maps of South America. Ask them to locate the map of South America in the atlas and study it closely. Then ask them to write down the names of all the countries in South America on paper.

Next, assign students to label on the blank outline map the countries of the continent. They can also locate and mark the capital cities.

Lesson 2:

Assemble ingredients and materials. Show students how to make a three-dimensional contour map of South America. Depending on the age level of your class, you may choose to make the medium home by yourself because it involves using boiling water. The following is a guide on how to make your own sawdust paste medium.

Materials:
6 large heat-proof mixing bowls
6 large wooden spoons
Cardboard pieces cut to the same size as the outline maps, enough for every student
6 heat-proof measuring cups
Several rag towels or paper towels for wipe-ups
3 electric kettles
A class set of plastic knives
Liquid tempera paint of different colors
6 size-8 round brushes and 6 size-10 flat brushes

Ingredients:
8 cups of all-purpose flour
8 cups of sifted fine sawdust (Obtainable at lumber store)
7 cups of boiling water
3 tablespoons salt

Directions:
Divide your class into working groups of no more than five.
Each student will take turn kneading the dough.
Equip each group with bowl, spoon, and measuring cup.
Teacher demonstrates method for whole class to observe.

Method:
1. Boil a kettle of water.
2. Mix dry ingredients well in mixing bowl.
3. Add boiling water to the dry mixture.
4. Stir well with wooden spoon to consistency of bread dough.

5. When wet mixture cools down, knead well with hands. Caution: Inside of dough may still be scalding hot.

6. When mixed well, use as soon as possible. Unused dough may be kept in refrigerator, wrapped in a plastic bag, for a week.

Lesson 3:   (If teacher makes dough at home, this is Lesson 2)

Ask students to paste outline maps on cardboard pieces provided. Allow two hours for them to dry. Provide students with strong book-binding tape and ask them to tape the four edges of the cardboard map down. Next, ask students to color the oceans blue.

Lesson 4:

Apply a layer (approximately a half-inch thick) of sawdust dough on the outlined continent, being careful not to have dough on the ocean parts of the map. With reference to a topographical map of South America found in the atlas, students will sculpt the land mass of the continent with some degree of approximation to the topographical information shown on the atlas map.

The members of the working group will have fun taking turns sculpting the land mass. More medium can be added if necessary while work is in progress. When the groups are satisfied with their three-dimensional maps, they may place them on a counter or on the floor to the side of the classroom for several days of drying.

Lesson 5:

Provide each group with liquid tempera paint and painting brushes. Instruct them to color their contour maps with appropriate colors in accordance to map-making conventions, i.e., blue for water, green for lowland, and as land elevation increases, ochre yellow, and different shades of brown are used, with the darkest shade for the highest land elevation.

Allow the finished products to dry. By the end of these lessons, students will have an intimate knowledge of the continent of South America. They will know the birthplace of Pablo Neruda.

Food Experience

15. Recipe

Though nutritionally balanced, this tasty pastry is generally served as an appetizer.

Empanadas

Ingredients:
    Dough (see below)
    Filling (see below)
    Olives (1 or 2 per student)
    Raisins (4 or 6 per student)
    Hard boiled eggs (1 egg for 2 to 4 students)

Dough:
5 cups flour
2 teaspoons baking powder
1 teaspoon salt
1/4 pound lard
1 cup milk

Filling:
4 onions chopped
1/2 cup oil
1 tablespoon paprika
1 pound ground beef
salt
oregano
pepper
1 bouillon cube dissolved in 1/2 cup of water
3 eggs, hard-boiled

1. Prepare filling
     a. Fry onion in hot oil until soft and transparent.
     b. Add paprika and ground beef, cooking till browned.
     c. Add remaining spices and bouillon.
     d. Simmer for 5 to 10 minutes on low heat.
     e. Cool.
2. Prepare dough
     a. Sift flour, baking powder and salt together.
     b. Add melted lard and hot milk, mixing well, but not kneading.
     c. Let stand for 20 minutes
     d. Roll it.
     e. Cut in circles approximately 8 inches (20 cm) in diameter.
3. Place in each circle one tablespoon filling, one olive, two or three raisins, one slice of hard-boiled egg.
4. Moisten the edges and fold, shaping them as triangles or rectangles.
5. Brush with egg white or milk. Puncture in 2 or 3 spots.
6. Place on a baking sheet and bake for 40 minutes at 375 F.
Note: To make classroom time less hectic for you, you may choose to prepare the dough and filling ahead and let the students assemble and bake their own empanadas. You may need to double or triple the recipe depending on your class size. If you do so, make each batch separately to ensure consistent results, especially with the dough.

Internet Resources

16. *http://www.tezcat.com/~carlhurt/LatinoAmerica.html*

This site includes a photo of Neruda and two of his poems, "Walking Around" and "Oda al Piano," as well as information about other poets.

17. *http://www.uchile.cl/WWW/nerudaing.html*

The University of Chile maintains this site. Here you can find a biography with photos of Neruda at various ages and an audio recording of Neruda reading two poems in Spanish. More information is available here about Pablo Neruda for those who can read Spanish.

18. *http://www.wco.com/~altaf/pablo.txt*

Contains "some thoughts on Pablo Neruda's epic poem 'The Heights of Macchu Picchu,'" and a biography.

Teacher's Notes

Alfred Nobel

Alfred was born in Stockholm in 1833. His father was a successful engineer and inventor as well. All through his young life, Alfred was provided with the best education to become a brilliant young scientist like his father.

Alfred spent many years of his life perfecting a volatile liquid explosive, nitroglycerine, which had been invented by an Italian chemist, Ascanio Sobrero. He developed the more stable form of explosive, coined dynamite, for rock drilling. He also invented a detonator that could be ignited by lighting a fuse.

These inventions drastically reduced the cost and time required in blasting rocks, drilling tunnels, building canals, and other forms of construction work. The market for dynamite and detonation caps grew rapidly, and Alfred Nobel proved himself to be a very enterprising industrialist. In slightly over 20 years, Alfred founded factories and laboratories in 90 different places throughout Europe, many of which are still in operation today. Some prominent examples are Imperial Chemical Industries (ICI) in Great Britain, Societe Centrale de Dynamite in France, and Dyno Industries in Norway.

Alfred's secretary and good friend, Countess Bertha von Suttner, a peace activist pioneer, was credited for influencing Alfred's dedication towards founding the Nobel Prize for recognizing contributions to mankind. It is now plain why the Nobel Prize recognizes the vastly divergent fields of human endeavor because Alfred Nobel was himself a truly "Renaissance Man." By the time of his death in 1896, Nobel received 355 patents. Bertha von Suttner was awarded the first Nobel Peace Prize by the Norwegian Parliament in 1905.

Bibliography

Allen, Leslie, "Tierra del Fuego," *Secret Corners of the World*, National Geographic Society (Washington, D.C.), 1982. "Less than 700 miles from Antarctica, Tierra del Fuega brings the Americas to a ragged end below the Straight of Magellan." Cape Horn, one island of this archipelago used to see much more traffic than it has since the Panama Canal opened, but life goes on and the scenery is breathtaking.

Arriaza, Bernardo, "Chile's Chinchorro Mummies," *National Geographic*, March 1995. May be too frightening for young children. This article looks at how the mummies were made and what the Chinchorro culture in Chile must have been like.

Boraiko, Allen A., "Acts of Faith in Chile," *National Geographic*, July 1988. Written when Chile was still governed by a military junta, the article gives an excellent picture of the political climate that prohibited Chilean citizens from paying tribute to Pablo Neruda for 17 years. A page-sized map and many color photos makes this an excellent resource.

Childcraft: The How and Why Library, Volume 4: *World and Space*. This volume contains information about deserts and tidal waves that would be useful for the science activities.

"Deserts," *The Young Children's Encyclopedia*, Volume 4. Encyclopaedia Britannica, Inc. (Chicago), 1977. This series of articles looks at camel trains as a way to cross the desert, nomads of the deserts, and desert life.

Duran, Manuel and Margery Safir, *Earth Tones: The Poetry of Pablo Neruda*, Indiana University Press (Bloomington), 1981. The authors focus on those works of Neruda that make up the critical movements in his career and those best known to his readers outside Chile. A biography, pictures, and a 16-page "selected" bibliography of Neruda's life and work are included.

"Fishing Industry," *Growing up with Science: The Illustrated "Encyclopedia of Invention, Volume 6*. H.S. Stuttman Inc. (Westport, Connecticut), 1984. An excellent resource for the science activity on fishing, this article includes photographs, diagrams, and information on finding the fish, netting the fish, types of nets used, navigation, work on the trawler, and factory ships.

Jacobsen, Karen, *A New True Book: Chile*, Childrens Press (Chicago), 1991. Learn about life in Chile, the different regions, the political upheaval of the 1970s and '80s, and the country's history. Illustrated. Grade 1+.

Miller, Jack, "Chile's Uncharted Cordillera Sarmiento," *National Geographic*, April 1994. A team of six attempt to conquer the unascended mountains on a peninsula west of Puerto Natales in southern Chile, but are beaten by a vicious wind.

Neruda, Pablo, *Art of Birds*, University of Texas Press (Austin), 1985. In English only, the poems are accompanied by pen and ink drawings. "Magellanic Penguin" gives praise to this stiff bird of the snow; "Black-Necked Swan" is a two-line poem. Could the class create other two-line poems about birds, following this style?

Neruda, Pablo, *Extravagaria*, Farrar, Straus, and Giroux (New York), 1974. Bilingual poems. Your younger students may be enthralled with the poem-story "Furious Struggle Between Seamen and an Octopus of Colossal Size." Or read to your class "Through a Closed Mouth the Flies Enter," which is full of couplets asking why, where, and when. You could ask students to write their own couplets with the answers.

Neruda, Pablo, *Five Decades: A Selection (Poems: 1925–1970)*, Grove Press (New York), 1974. Bilingual. If your students are fluent in both languages, have them compare the lines of Spanish to the lines of English and decide if they agree with the English translation. If your students are not fluent in Spanish, ask them to identify words and phrases they recognize or can figure out.

Neruda, Pablo, *Late and Posthumous Poems: 1968–1974*, Grove Press (New York), 1988. Bilingual. Young children will love the questions Neruda poses in the lengthy poem "Question Book," and older students will appreciate the play on words. Can your class add more questions to this poem?

Neruda, Pablo. *Odes to Opposites*. Little Brown (Boston), 1995.

Neruda, Pablo. *Odes to Common Things.* Harcourt (New York), 1992. These odes are about everyday events in children's lives. Ask your students to write an ode to a commonplace thing like a crayon, a desk, or a shoe.

Neruda, Pablo, *Passions and Impressions*, Farrar, Straus and Giroux (New York), 1983. A book of prose, with each story or commentary only a page or two long. Choose several to read to your intermediate class. They might particularly enjoy "My Name is Crusoe."

Neruda, Pablo, *Toward the Splendid City: Nobel Lecture*, Farrar, Straus and Giroux (New York), 1972. If only all lectures were this interesting! Grades 6 and up might enjoy having this very short book read aloud to them. Bilingual.

Posel, Elsa, "The True Book of Deserts," *I Want to Know About..., Volume 9*. Childrens Press (Chicago), 1972. Beginning readers learn here about what a desert is, where deserts are found, what plants and animals live in the desert, and the kinds of people who live there as well.

"Robinson Crusoe's Island," *Disney's Wonderful World of Knowledge Yearbook 1978*. Danbury Press (Danbury, Connecticut), 1978. The Juan Fernandez Islands belong to Chile, and the one known as Robinson Crusoe's is inhabited by about 700 people. But back in the beginning of the 1700s, Alexander Selkirk lived here for more than four years alone. Daniel Dafoe based *Robinson Crusoe* on Selkirk's experiences.

Roman, Joseph. *Pablo Neruda*, Chelsea House (New York), 1992. This is a biography of Neruda for older students.

"Tsunami," *Growing up with Science: The Illustrated Encyclopedia of Invention, Volume 19*. H.S. Stuttman (Westport, Connecticut) 1984. What are tsunamis? How are they formed? Where do they occur? This article will answer these questions and more.

Wall 14 Community Graffiti Abatement: Fighting Crime with Art

Pre-Reading Warm-Up

1. Is Graffiti Art? Is Art Crime an Oxymoron?

The pro-graffiti camp argues that graffiti is art of the people. They boldly admit that graffiti art is "art crime." They also advocate that the community should provide "legal" walls so that they may perform their brand of visual art.

What is Graffiti? Why is it done? who does it? "Is graffiti art?" is a good topic for debate by students. Hold a discussion of the pros and cons of graffiti, so that opposing debating teams may be equally prepared for their arguments. Your students might want to invite some local artists to participate in these discussions.

Language Arts

2. Editorial Writing

Why, or why not, should graffiti be disallowed? Let the students choose sides and explain in writing their opinions. Several editorials could be sent to the local newspaper as a letter to the editor, or they could be posted so that others could read them.

3. Debate the Issue of Graffiti

Select three or four students each for two teams to debate this: "Graffiti is an art." The other students can be the audience and vote on who made the better case. This is an opportunity to introduce debating techniques, of which much information is available.

4. Letter Writing and E-Mailing

To express your appreciation and encouragement to the environmental and community initiatives developed everywhere, ask your students to write to these project organizations and show your support.

Philadelphia Anti-Graffiti Network (PAGN)
Timothy Spencer,
1220 Sansom Street, Third Floor,
Philadelphia, PA 19107
USA
Ph. (215) 686-1550; Fax (215) 686-1564

The Union-Tribune Solutions
Karen Lin Clark, Editor,
The San Diego Union-Tribune,
P.O.Box 191,
San Diego, CA 92112
USA
Ph. (619) 293-1317
E-mail address: *utsolv@aol.com*

The Anti-Graffiti Project,
The National Council to Prevent Delinquency
P.O.Box 16675, Dept. NPCA,
Alexandria, VA 22301-8675,
USA
Ph. (703) 751-9569; Fax (703) 751-3507

Committee for a Better North Philadelphia
Mr. Tyrone Reed, Executive Director,
1401 West York Street,
Philadelphia, PA 19132
USA
Ph. (215) 225-1990 and 225-8886

The Global Garden Plot
National Round Table on the Environment and the Economy,
1 Nicholas Street, Suite 1500,
Ottawa, Ontario
Canada, K1N 7B7
Ph. (613) 992-7189; Fax (613) 992-7385

Social Studies

5. Graffiti as a Social Problem

Discuss with your class the ways in which the graffiti sub-culture may be linked to youth gang sub-cultures. Invite a police officer from the youth crime unit to speak to your class about this issue. Is there graffiti in your area? What is it? Why is it there?

6. Laws Against Graffiti

In California, victims of graffiti vandalism may take the parents of minors who are responsible for the crime, to court for damages. Parents are liable under the California Civil Code for reimbursement to victims of vandalism up to $25,000.

Are there local legislations that outlaw graffiti vandalism in your city? Assign students to find out.

7. The Graffiti Sub-Culture

Graffiti artists' tools include paint, spray paint, shoe polish, magic markers, scratching/etching tools, stickers, grease pencils, ink, and chalk. They work both at night and daytime, generally on weekends and school holidays.

Favorite targets are traffic signs, freeway signs, light poles, electrical boxes, fences, utility boxes, bus stops, bus shelters, sidewalk benches, and walls. Recently, there is a new form of graffiti that involves scratching messages and tags (stylized signatures) onto glass, plastic, or other surfaces. This form of vandalism creates a particular hazard because a large glass surface, such as a shop window, becomes weakened when etched, and it may shatter and collapse at the slightest movement or vibration. When a large window breaks, people are placed at great risk.

Like an artist, the graffiti "artist" leaves his/her signature in the form of a stylized personal logo, a "tag," as it is called. They adopt the curious lingo of the graffiti underworld. Some examples are: a "writer" is a practitioner of graffiti art; a "piece" is a graffiti painting, short for masterpiece; and "to piece" means to paint graffiti.

Ask your students to notice graffiti as they see one and to note its characteristics. Provide your class with an opportunity to share their observations. Write their observations on chart paper and discuss any possible patterns.

Science

8. Community Gardens

Are there community gardens in your city or town? Where are they? Arrange for your class to help out for a day or a week or a few hours per week for several weeks. No community garden? Why not do what the Herons did (see "Earth Day: 25 Years" in the bibliography at the end of this chapter)? Get permission from your town or city to turn a vacant lot near the school into a garden that the whole school and/or community can help nurture. Perhaps you could find a volunteer from among the parents to head such a project.

Mathematics

9. Data Management of Graffiti

Assign an action research assignment in which students, with the permission and help of their parents, go around their community, either on foot or by car, and identify specific locations of graffiti. Give them a week so that they may have a chance to conduct some "sightseeing" tours of their immediate community with their parents.

On a sheet of chart paper, construct a large bar graph which visually presents the size of the graffiti problem in your community.

10. Data Management of Mural Painting

In many communities in North America, graffiti abatement efforts take on a positive and active tone. With funding from municipal governments and/or members of the local community, mural art is used to cover up violent and unsavory messages that graffiti-artists attempted to convey.

Like the activity suggested above, organize and conduct field trips to locate mural paintings in your community. Enter the mural painting information on a bar graph with reference to the number of paintings in specific locations. The graph would serve to tell the story of how your community has been dealing with the problem of graffiti.

Arts and Crafts

11. The Mural Art Movement of Diego Rivera

Modern-day mural art can be attributed to the enthusiasm and efforts of a Mexican artist, Diego Rivera. For years, Rivera painted wall murals to depict both the hardship of the average Mexican and the glories of Mexican history.

Refer to a chapter on Diego Rivera's mural painting in *Talking Walls* by Margy Burns Knight, published by Tilbury House, Publishers in1992. Many teaching ideas are found in its companion *Teacher's Guide*.

12. Mural Painting: An Art Activity

Tape a long sheet of white art-project paper (comes in a roll) onto the gymnasium wall. Ask students to sketch in pencil scenes of school life. Provide students with liquid tempera paint, paint brushes, empty cans for paint, Styrofoam trays for mixing colors, cans of water, and paper towels. Ask them to paint the mural by filling in and embellishing their sketches.

Leave the mural up for a week so that the whole school will have a chance to see it. It would be an appropriate mural to be displayed for a school-wide event such as "Meet The Teacher Night" at the beginning of the school year or the end-of-the-year graduation. (The mural could also be the blueprint for the following activity)

13. Social Participation: A School-Community "Paint Out" Project

"The difference between graffiti and art is permission."

If there is graffiti in the immediate vicinity of the school, seek the approval of your school administrator, parents, municipal officials, and local businesses for a community anti-graffiti "Paint Out." You may need to organize a school and community meeting to clearly detail your objectives and action plans.

With donations from local paint and decoration businesses, obtain the necessary tools for mural painting. With an interested group, brainstorm appropriate themes for mural art in the school community. Provide students with ample opportunities for practice with sketching on art paper. (The previous activity could provide the students with a trial run.)

Designate a day as Community Beautification Day when the "Paint Out" will take place with fanfare. Invite local media to capture your school's effort in painting out unsightly graffiti and replacing it with the uplifting themes of mural art. This kind of community-minded spirit and cooperative effort is the goal of civic responsibility in the social studies curriculum.

Food Experience

14. Recipe

There is no food that represents the issue of graffiti. However, you might want to try this as a comparative food experience for your students. Using two large cakes, decorate one with graffiti and the other with more attractive art. Few schools have available to them pans large enough for slab cakes. You may choose to order two un-iced slab cakes from a bakery or divide your class into four groups and have each group mix and bake one cake (two cakes would then be joined to form one cake). Since it takes several hours for cakes to cool completely (which must occur before icing), you may decide to have the students bake the cake one day and decorate on the second day.

Graffiti Cakes

Cake:

Ingredients:

2/3 cup butter or margarine, softened	2-3/4 cups all-purpose flour
1-3/4 cups sugar	2-1/2 teaspoons baking powder
2 eggs	1 teaspoon salt
1-1/2 teaspoons vanilla	1-1/4 cups milk

Method:

1. Heat oven to 350 degrees Fahrenheit.
2. Grease and flour 13 by 9 inch baking pan.
3. In large mixing bowl, mix butter, sugar, eggs, and vanilla until light and fluffy. (If you have access to mixing machines, the job will be easy for the students but more dangerous because of the speed of the mixer. Alternatively each group can be given a wire whisk and the students can take turns whipping the ingredients until of the desired consistency.)
4. Beat 5 minutes on high speed if using an electric mixer, 10 minutes if beating by hand, scraping the bowl occasionally. (If using an electric mixer, turn it off before scraping.)
5. Combine dry ingredients into a different bowl.
6. On low speed, add a third of the dry ingredients to the butter mixture, till no flour is distinguishable.
7. Add half of the milk and mix at low speed until it is well mixed in.
8. Continue adding dry ingredients and milk alternately, ending with the dry.
9. Pour into pan.
10. Bake 45 to 50 minutes.
11. Cool

Icing

Each group will make one batch of white icing to cover the cake. Two batches will be used to cover the cakes and two will be divided, colored, and used to decorate. (Tubes of colored icing are available and may be used instead.)

Ingredients:

2/3 cup soft butter or margarine	1 tablespoon vanilla
6 cups confectioners' sugar (icing sugar)	1/4 cup (approximately) milk

Method:
1. Blend butter and sugar.
2. Stir in vanilla and milk.
3. Beat until icing is smooth and of spreading consistency.

Assembling
1. Place two cakes, long sides together, on a rigid surface (large tray, foil-covered cardboard etc.) joining them with icing in between (using it as glue).
2. Cover the entire two cakes with one batch of icing, making them look like one cake.
3. Repeat steps one and two for the other two cakes.
4. Divide the remaining icing into small bowls (1/2 cup approximately in each bowl) OR used purchased tubes of colored icing and skip steps five and six.
5. Add food coloring to make the desired colors (cocoa will make brown) and mix well.
6. Make your own icing tubes with CLEAN letter-sized envelopes: place about 1/4 cup icing in envelope, fold sides, and snip off a corner (not too much) to make a tip. Many of these can be made, each with a different color of icing inside.
7. Decorate the cakes with the colored icing. Two groups can combine to decorate one cake with the undesirable kind of graffiti (each student in that group should get a chance to do this), and the other cake can be decorated to illustrate a more favorable form of wall art. (Some practice with using the envelope-tubes may be needed. Roll down the "tube" from the top to push more icing out as you progress.)
8. Display the cakes for a day.
9. Share with other classes and eat!

Note: If graffiti is a problem in your neighborhood, you may wish to have your class to lead a school assembly in discussing the problems of graffiti and then share the cakes with all the students before they return to their classes.

Internet Resources

15. News Media Coverage of Graffiti Problem

If your school has access to Internet resources, you may direct your students to view recent and latest news coverage of the graffiti problem in *The San Francisco Chronicle, The San Francisco Examiner, San Jose Mercury News, The Houston Chronicle, San Diego Tribune,* and other news sources at this "Graffiti In The News" site. The URL is: *http://www.ccnet.com/~dougs/grnews.html*

16. The Philadelphia Anti-Graffiti Network

The Philadelphia story is a heart-warming one as it is more than a story of graffiti abatement. It is the success story of a community actualizing their common vision to turn idle minds into talented lives.

In 1984, Wilson Goode, the former Mayor of Philadelphia, launched the Anti-Graffiti Network under the artistic direction of Stanford University art graduate, Jane Golden. Its early aim was to paint over graffiti-covered walls in the city. Soon, the creativity of the Network members conceived of a mural art program designed to surpass mere graffiti removal to reforming delinquent youths by giving them a legitimate outlet for their creative expression.

Inspired by the artistic integrity of Mexican mural painters like Diego Rivera, Jane Golden, who coordinated the design and painting of over 1,300 murals in the city of Philadelphia, explained: "Mural painting is similar to graffiti in that it's big, it's outdoors, it's bold. We are dealing with a population of kids who are without a voice, and that's what they're searching for. That's what we're able to do: put their tag name all over town.... Our murals are very political. It creates a different world, and through that illusion, it provides a sense of hope."

More than 2,500 teenagers, some of whom are court-mandated to perform community services, take part in the Network each year. Most of the murals depict the daily struggles, triumphs, and tragedies of urban life. Some are dedicated to the ideals of North American culture embodied in cultural icons such as former baseball star, Julius Erving, Martin Luther King Jr., Harriet Tubman, and the late Mayor Frank Rizzo.

Organizers of the Network are quick to point out that 90% of the murals are untouched by hardcore graffiti vandals, as most of them hold an unspoken respect for the murals. The murals in Philadelphia are roses among thorns of graffiti, and they breath life into the city.

To view more than 30 photographs of murals painted in Philadelphia (many of them by the Anti-Graffiti Network), go to:
URL: *http://www.library.upenn.edu/~toccafondi/murals.html*

17. Pleasant Hill Graffiti Abatement

The problem of graffiti and how it is being handled in this community is discussed at length on the first page of this site:
URL: *http://www.ccnet.com/~dougs/phgraf.html*

At the bottom of the page are links to:
- Graffiti in the News;
- Alternatives to Graffiti (see below);
- Graffiti links on the World Wide Web (many, many resources available);
- Art Crimes (more than just an index of links to pro-graffiti sites, one question discussed is, "Is there a benefit to the study of graffiti as an art form instead of condemn it as vandalism?")
- More links.

18. Alternative Approaches to the Graffiti Problem

The question is asked, "Do we give in to the vandals or do we discover ways to help them understand there is more to life than aerosol paint, hate, and victimizing others?" It looks at solutions and alternatives to graffiti vandalism. Go to:
URL: *http://www.ccnet.com/~dougs/graalt.html*

Alternatives addressed include:
- Graffiti Abatement Activities such as:
    - Paint Brush Diplomacy (using art for world peace as an alternative to vandalism);
    - Ogontz Avenue Art Company (developed by Pete Doyle of Philadelphia who used his art and computer skills and passion for kids to transform neighborhoods);
    - Graffiti Grapplers of San Antonio, Texas ("Anson Jones Middle School fights community blight including graffiti");
    - Social Contract Project (of Philadelphia).
- Bay Area Youth Programs (two links available);
- National and Local Organizations Dedicated to Youth (plenty of links here);
- Things for young adults and kids to do besides victimize others (again, lots of links);
- Solutions (quite a few);
- Religious Community/Youth Out Reach (did you know there were so many?).

19. Another Success Story of Social Participation by School Children

The school community was tired of the graffiti-covered buildings, illegally dumped garbage, and vandalized fences and windows around the school neighborhood of Anson Jones Middle School in San Antonio, Texas. The staff and students of the school decided to do something about it in the spring of

1993. A science class grew into an environmental club which, in turn, became an effective youth project against graffiti and vandalism in the community. These are the famed Graffiti Grapplers of San Antonio, Texas!

The mission of the Grapplers was to reclaim and beautify the community by reducing the visual impact of gang graffiti and unsanitary and unsightly litter. The students, under adult supervision and with their assistance, whitewash graffiti-covered walls, fences, poles, and other vandalized objects. They pick up garbage in the neighborhood. The Grapplers were such a welcome and heartening sight to the local residents that they wrote them thank-you notes, and delivered snacks and drinks to the young volunteers while they worked. The group has become a Clean Texas 2000 partner and has received much formal recognition from government agencies and private corporations.

Please refer to "Teacher's Notes" for a sample of statements from the middle years students of Anson Jones Middle School. It would be most worthwhile for your class to correspond with the young crusaders of community contributors. The address of Anson Jones Middle School is: *1256 Pinn Road, San Antonio, TX 78227, USA*

You may also access the Internet story of the Graffiti Grapplers via the following:
URL: *http://www.tristero.com/sa/grapplers/*

At this site you can find:
*   An overview of the Grapplers' project;
*   Statements prepared for City Council meetings;
*   Kids' poems;
*   Hints on creating other Graffiti Grappler groups;
*   Photo album.

20. Paintbrush Diplomacy: A Children and Art Project

For over twenty years, this innovative project has aimed at bringing children of all ages around the world together through an exchange of artwork and letters. Over 14,000 children from eighty countries have participated in Paintbrush Diplomacy. The project has a permanent collection of 3,500 paintings for travelling exhibitions and publications. The present dream is to hold the first international children's art gallery in the U.S. For further information and participation, please go to:
URL: *http://newciv.org/worldtrans/BOV/BI/BI-12.HTML*

or write to:
Paintbrush Diplomacy
1717 17th Street,
San Francisco, CA 94103
USA
Ph. (415) 255-7478
Fax (415) 255-7479

Teacher's Notes
Statements from Student Graffiti Grapplers

"I am a Graffiti Grappler! Why, you ask? The reason is I do not like gang graffiti and trash in our parks and on our land. It's not fair for senior citizens to repaint their houses just because someone had nothing else better to do than to write on their fences and houses. I would like to see a cleaner San Antonio. I am willing to volunteer my time. Are you willing to volunteer time and supplies to keep San Antonio cleaner? It's not just senior citizens, but the children of San Antonio who depend on it!"

"Once I was a littering person—destroying the city and all. Day by day, trash by trash, was all that I saw. Until I opened my eyes and opened my ears and experienced what I've done. So I changed my ways and tried to do something about what we almost destroyed. I joined Graffiti Grapplers and now I try to beautify our city and I hope you do, too!"

"I enjoy being in Graffiti Grapplers because it makes me feel better about myself and my neighborhood. It also helps our neighborhood to be pretty. I also think it sets a good example for the younger kids. They see us doing this and they get involved, too. I do this because it makes us look better!"

"It just feels good to know you're doing something right. Even picking up a little piece of trash is helping!"

"Last year I was fortunate enough to belong to the Graffiti Grapplers. As a member of this group, I learned how wonderful it feels to take responsibility for caring about our environment. It means a lot to me to be an active part of the community and to lend a helping hand in making our world a better place."

"Graffiti Grapplers are kids showing pride and self-respect, and to have a chance to show others that teenagers can be good and responsible citizens, too."

"We want to remind everyone to be more aware of the habits that affect the well-being of our planet. Take a minute to think before throwing that paper out of the car window; take rubbish to the appropriate land fill or hazardous waste center; recycle at every opportunity; help a neighbor when things get tough; report code compliance violations that go untended; become people who take action to solve problems, not just people who talk about them."

Chemainus: The Little Town That Did

Chemainus is a small community situated just north of Victoria, the capital of British Columbia, on Vancouver Island. Several years ago, the town's industries and economy took a drastic downturn. People were leaving town. To save Chemainus from becoming a ghost town, the residents worked hard to revive the town through a massive mural campaign. The buildings in the entire community of Chemainus were beautified with murals of historic scenes from around this area of British Columbia. Overnight, Chemainus became a tourist sensation. The little town that did.

Two local Chemainus mural artists, Dan and Peter Sawatsky, impressed the touring Americans so much that they were commissioned to paint an 80 x 14' mural at the entrance to Twentynine Palms, California, recreating the spirit of the hearty folk who helped settled the American West. For more information about quality mural painting projects, call Twentynine Palms, CA 92277 at (619) 361-2286.

Bibliography

Graham, Frank Jr., "Earth Day: 25 Years," *National Geographic*, April 1995. Percy and Ella Heron have taken a vacant lot, full of garbage, turned it into the jewel of the neighborhood, and use it to teach children about the soil and water.

Greenburg, Keith Elliot, *Out of the Gang*, Lerner Publications (Minneapolis), 1995. Graffiti and gangs often seem to go together. Gino and Butch are two boys who grew up in a rough New York neighborhood. Butch joined a gang and paid a heavy price later to get out of it. Gino vowed at an early age to stay out of gangs and now helps to cover up graffiti. Grade 4+.

Tamar, Erika, *The Garden of Happiness*, Harcourt Brace (New York), 1996. Children help plant a garden in a vacant lot. Marisol plants a special seed and older children paint a mural that surprises her.

More Books by Margy Burns Knight, illustrated by Anne Sibley O'Brien, and Teacher's Guides by Margy Burns Knight and Thomas V. Chan

Talking Walls: The Stories Continue The world is full of interesting walls, from the mighty dikes that keep the ocean from flooding the Netherlands, to the Wall of Messages outside the home of Chile's beloved poet, Pablo Neruda, to the Peace Lines separating Catholic and Protestant neighborhoods in Belfast, Ireland. Beautifully illustrated with the vibrant color pastels of Anne Sibley O'Brien, these stories help us explore and understand the diversity of our world, its issues, and its people. Hardcover, $17.95, English (ISBN 0-88448-164-6). English paperback available in Fall, 1997.

Las paredes hablan: Cuentan más historias [*Talking Walls: The Stories Continue*] Spanish translation by Clarita Kohen, Hardcover, $17.95 (ISBN 0-88448-166-2). Paperback, $8.95 (ISBN 0-88448-167-0).

Talking Walls "Pick of the Lists," *American Bookseller*, 1995; *Booklist* Starred Review; Featured Title in the ABC *Building Blocks* catalog; named by the *Boston Globe* as one of the Top 25 Non-Fiction Children's Books of 1992; finalist for *Hungry Mind Review* Children's Books of Distinction. *Talking Walls* Introduces young readers to different cultures by exploring the stories of walls around the world and how they separate or hold communities together. Hardcover, $17.95 (ISBN 0-88448-102-6). Paperback, $8.95 (ISBN 0-88448-154-9).

Las paredes hablen [*Talking Walls*] Spanish translation by Clarita Kohen. Hardcover, $17.95 (ISBN 0-88448-156-5). Paperback, $8.95 (ISBN 0-88448-157-3).

Talking Walls Teacher's Guide, with Thomas V. Chan. Features over 200 imaginative lessons in geography, language, poetry, world cultures, ethnic heritage, religion, rituals, science, math, art, and architecture. Saddlestitched, $9.95 (ISBN 0-88448-106-9).

Who Belongs Here? An American Story "Best Multicultural Book," 1993 *Publishers Weekly* "Cuffie Award" and a 1993 "Pick of the List," *American Booksellers*. *Who Belongs Here?* tells the story of Nary, a young boy from Cambodia who flees for his life from civil war in his homeland. In the United States at last, he can scarcely believe the freedom and safety he enjoys, and yet to some of his classmates he is a "chink, " a "gook" who should "Get back on the boat" and go back where he belongs. But what if everyone who now lives in the U.S., but whose ancestors came from another country, was forced to return to his or her homeland. Who would be left? This book teaches empathy for recent immigrants by exploring our common history as immigrants. Hardcover, $16.95 (ISBN 0-88448-110-7). Paperback, $8.95, (ISBN 0-88448-169-7).

¿Quién es de aquí? Una historia americana [*Who Belongs Here?*] Spanish translation by Clarita Kohen. Hardcover, $16.95 (ISBN O-88448-158-1). Paperback, $8.95 (ISBN 0-88448-159-X).

Who Belongs Here? Teacher's Guide, with Thomas V. Chan. This activity guide for classroom teachers and homeschool parents helps students explore immigration, repatriation, refugees, tolerance, and other topics related to diversity. Saddlestitched, $9.95 (ISBN 0-88448-111-5).

Welcoming Babies "Beginning with its endpapers covered with babies in their amazing variety, *Welcoming Babies* is a celebration of the beginnings of life for humans.... Besides being an excellent multicultural title, expectant families can use this as a read-aloud...." —*The Bulletin of the Center for Children's Books*. Hardcover, $14.95 (ISBN 0-88448-123-9).

Welcoming Diversity, our quarterly newsletter for educators, is free upon request.

For more information about these books and about "Telling Our Stories" workshops with Margy Burns Knight and Anne Sibley O'Brien, or workshops with Thomas V. Chan (in Canada) go to our web page: **http://www.tilburyhouse.com** or contact:

Tilbury House, Publishers • 2 Mechanic Street • Gardiner, ME 04345
800–582–1899 – fax 207–582–8227 • email tilbury@tilburyhouse.com

Notes

Notes

Notes